Visions and Revisions

Visions and Revisions
Ethnohistoric Perspectives
on Southern Cultures

George Sabo III and William M. Schneider,
Editors

Southern Anthropological Society Proceedings, No. 20
Mary W. Helms, Series Editor

The University of Georgia Press
Athens and London

Southern Anthropological Society

Founded 1966

© 1987 by the Southern Anthropological Society
Published by the University of Georgia Press
Athens, Georgia 30602
All rights reserved

Set in 11 on 13 Times Roman
The paper in this book meets the guidelines for permanence and durability of the Committee on Production Guidelines for Book Longevity of the Council on Library Resources.

Printed in the United States of America

91 90 89 88 87   5 4 3 2 1

Library of Congress Cataloging in Publication Data

Visions and revisions.

(Southern Anthropological Society proceedings; no. 20)
Papers presented at a symposium held at the 1985 meeting of the Southern Anthropological Society in Fayetteville, Ark.
1. Ethnology—Southern States—Congresses.
2. Southern States—Antiquities—Congresses.
3. Southern States—Social life and customs—Congresses.
4. Indians of North America—Southern States—Congresses. I. Sabo, George. II. Schneider, William M. III. Southern Anthropological Society. Meeting. IV. Series.
GN2.S9243   no. 20   [F220.A1]   306'.0975   86-16043
ISBN 0-8203-0911-7 (alk. paper)
ISBN 0-8203-0912-5 (pbk.: alk. paper)

Contents

Visions and Revisions

Introduction

George Sabo III and William M. Schneider

The papers in this volume were originally presented in the key symposium "Ethnohistoric Perspectives on the South" held at the 1985 Southern Anthropological Society meeting in Fayetteville, Arkansas. One symposium participant, Melanie L. Sovine, unfortunately was not able to submit her paper, entitled "Withington Station and Withering Missions: An Ethnohistorical Perspective on Baptist Missions and Indian Removal in the American South" for publication in this volume.

Our initial intention was to explore issues concerning organization and change in southern cultures using ethnohistoric approaches that rely on documentary materials. Several of the papers presented at the meeting and published here do indeed rely on documents as primary sources of ethnographic data. These papers illustrate the many perspectives now used in anthropology to gain insight into the past via these sources. Additionally, these studies explore significantly different expressions of interaction between past and present among different cultural groups in the South. In hindsight, the identification and interpretation of these expressions seem to be the most salient contributions of the symposium. It also became apparent to us that an important part of how we both as anthropologists and Southerners view southern culture has to do with the cognitive-cultural screens with which we sift the information about the past available to us. Many of the papers in this volume, therefore, pursue the issue of cultural interaction between the past and the present. Our commentary in this introduction summarizes each paper with respect to these issues.

De Soto's epic journey across the southeastern United States is reexamined in Hudson's paper, in which he uses the ideas of French social historian Fernand Braudel (1980) to illuminate the sixteenth-century South. Hudson exhorts us to bridge the gap between history and anthropology through attention to "structural phenomena of long duration." This is a different kind of structuralism, but on reflection it seems akin to the Lévi-Straussian model prevalent in anthropology and used in other papers in this volume. Hudson's use of Braudel's model emphasizes the social, demographic, and environmental and leaves us but a short step from the cognitive perspective. Hudson further shows how such a structural analysis allows us to reinterpret the records of European travels in the Southeast from a cultural perspective, adding an important new dimension to the anthropological interpretation of history.

Sabo's analysis of Caddoan culture at the time of European contact and the impact of that contact from the perspective of the Caddoan uses an interpretive model developed by Sahlins in his work on the Hawaiians and Captain Cook (Sahlins 1981). In this model historical events are mediated by the cultural categories of the participants, and through the interaction of these categories across cultural boundaries structural transformations result. The Caddoan contact experience is interpreted in terms of Caddoan world view and the effort to maintain the preexisting cognitive structures and accommodate the impact of the contact experience. This approach provides an enhanced understanding of Caddoan culture before, during, and after European contact and of the contact experience itself.

During the nineteenth century a large number of Cherokee settled in Arkansas, but after only a few decades they were removed to Indian Territory in present-day Oklahoma. The paper by Davis addresses the archeological visibility of past Cherokee settlement in Arkansas. Although much of the area formerly occupied is now inundated by large man-made reservoirs, there remain many areas where Cherokee sites could still exist. What would these sites consist of, and would archeologists be able to identify these separately from sites of contemporaneous white settlers? These are difficult problems since the Arkansas Cherokee were economically acculturated by the time they moved into Arkansas. Davis argues, however, that certain aspects of Cherokee culture remained distinctive, including the form of community organization and settlement and communal activities such as ball games and other contests. These phenomena would probably not be recognized at the individual site level, but a regional archeological focus might well identify an overall settlement pattern exhibiting ethnically distinctive characteristics.

Stewart-Abernathy examines what he calls the Ozark Tradition Myth through an analysis of the archeological remains of a turn-of-the-century northwest Arkansas farmstead, coupled with additional information derived from oral and written sources. The popular cultural image of the isolated, independent, backward Ozark hillbilly is an important part of our historical view of the region and therefore plays a role in determining our actions and interpretations of others in today's world. But the Moser farmstead data cause us to rethink our image of the traditional Ozarker. Independence and self-sufficiency were important values held by nineteenth- and early twentieth-century Ozarkers, but these were not maintained through isolation and they need not imply backwardness. In this treatment documents of several kinds are used not only to inform an interpretation of the past but to provide a critique of popular contemporary images of that same past.

The analysis of settlement patterns in the Current River Valley of southeast Missouri by Price demonstrates important differences in pattern between the upper and lower parts of the valley. The small, dispersed farms and lack of settlement nucleation of the upper valley provide a contrast to the larger farms, towns, and manufacturing centers present in the lower valley. Using a variety of documentary sources Price shows that economic, environmental, and historical factors all seem to have been important in generating the contrast between these locales. The Current River Valley is thus shown to be a microcosm in which the hill/lowland contrast present in the South as a region may be examined in detail and for which anthropological explanations may be sought.

In a very interesting paper on early twentieth-century lynchings in southwest Missouri, Purrington and Harter deal with the role of newspapers in reflecting and shaping perceptions of blacks and race relations built on these perceptions. Examination of newspaper accounts of lynchings in Springfield and Joplin before, during, and after the events allows an understanding of the cultural milieu and the cognitive framework in which the lynchings occurred. Here the documentary sources themselves—the newspaper accounts—rather than the events are the focus of interpretation. Newspapers are themselves a special cultural category and by recognizing this Purrington and Harter are able to demonstrate how atavistic images of blacks, however misbegotten, have endured as part of the local cognitive/social structure. Though the brutal events of the past remain locked in that time frame, the interpretation and meaning of these events have been carried along by enduring cognitive categories. This, in the words of the authors, "helps us better understand why blacks play such a limited role in the region today."

The Schneiders' treatment of the Chinese grocery store in the Mississippi Delta is an avowedly structural one that interprets the apparently anomalous Chinese store in terms of peculiarly southern social and cognitive structures. The Chinese merchants fit so well in the economic and social structure of delta communities because of their liminal status between the black and white segments of the binary southern caste system. The structuralist perspective allows us to see that the alien Chinese slipped into an economic, social, and cognitive niche awaiting them or other immigrants much as the European Jews did in some other areas of the South. The analysis was developed largely upon interviews with delta inhabitants—white, black, and Chinese. Cognitive categories and structures persisting to the present thus provide a frame within which historical information on the Chinese grocery store is interpreted. Although the problem and approach to analysis are synchronic, this paper documents an enduring social structure and offers an explanation for its persistence.

The treatment of Bethel Methodist Camp Meeting by Rees in terms of the relationship between archaism and the physical layout of the campground is most insightful. Rees illuminates the meaning of the camp meeting and its setting for the participants by analyzing differential placement of items of modern technology (automobiles, campers, and so forth) and more traditional artifacts around the campground. Sacred and profane activities are also organized with respect to the layout of the campground. The unique meaning of Bethel Camp Meeting is thus seen to lie more in the spatial organization of artifacts and behaviors than in the overt religious activities which occur there. But embodied in the spatial layout, and thus an important part of its meaningfulness, are values and traditions of the past which also figure significantly in the present religious beliefs of the participants. Thus the Bethel Camp Meeting actively makes use of the past to give meaning to present religious belief. Moreover, this unique interaction between past and present is illuminated not by the interpretation of written documents but by studying the camp and its arrangement as a "document" of a very different sort.

In summary, the papers contained in this volume treat a variety of southern cultures from a variety of historical perspectives. These treatments certainly do not exhaust the theoretical and methodological possibilities for ethnohistoric synthesis, as Peacock points out in his concluding commentary. They do bring together a number of valuable perspectives based on concepts drawn from anthropology which may usefully be applied to the analysis and interpretation of the past. And we learn from these treatments that an important aspect of historical interpretation is the manner in which categories and structures from the past interact with those of the present. This interaction is both a process mediating historical interpretation as well as a historic process itself amenable to anthropological analysis. Here especially, it seems, is where further ethnohistoric efforts may be directed.

The anthropological study of history is a vibrant and growing field. We believe the papers presented here provide a valuable contribution to the study of southern cultures and we hope they will stimulate further reflection and growth.

REFERENCES

Braudel, Fernand, 1980. History and Social Sciences: The *Longue Durée*. In *On History,* Fernand Braudel (Chicago: University of Chicago Press), pp. 25–54.

Sahlins, Marshall, 1981. *Historical Metaphors and Mythic Realities, Structure in the Early History of the Sandwich Islands Kingdom* (Ann Arbor: The University of Michigan Press).

An Unknown South: Spanish Explorers and Southeastern Chiefdoms

Charles Hudson

My purpose here is to argue that an entire century needs to be added to the history of the American South, and that southern anthropologists have a crucial role to play in doing this.[1] The century I have in mind is not the seventeenth century, which has suffered relative neglect but nonetheless been the subject of considerable specialist research from time to time. This is not to say that the history of the seventeenth-century South cannot be improved or that anthropologists have no role to play in improving it.[2] Much work remains to be done, for example, on the Spanish mission systems among the Indians of the lower South and even more on Indian societies in the interior. But if there are gaps in our understanding of the seventeenth-century South, the sixteenth century is, for all practical purposes, simply missing from southern history.[3] It is a century in which there is little more than the history of a few famous Europeans—Ponce de Leon and Hernando de Soto, primarily. It is a century in which the South is merely a piece of *terra incognita* in the "age of exploration." Or if it does take any shape at all, it is as a not very important part of the "Spanish borderlands." From this perspective it is seen as one of the areas in North America in which Spain maintained only a token presence and over which she exerted an uncertain control in competition with France and England (Bannon 1974).

The sixteenth-century South has received its most definite shape through the researches of archeologists, who are rather more interested in the Indians than in exploring Spaniards or border Spaniards. Archeologists have in recent decades added immeasurably to our fund of information on the Indians of this century. But southern archeologists have, for the most part, written for other archeologists. They have not been much concerned with communicating what they have learned to scholars in other fields, much less to laymen.

The sixteenth-century Southeast was neither an empty stage nor simply a borderland where rival colonial powers fought for supremacy, and the human drama that unfolded there is too important to be obscured by specialist language. The story of the sixteenth-century South is the story of a vigorous land of Indian chiefdoms, the most advanced societies in North America, which had evolved on southern soil as a result of an important social transformation that began back in the ninth century A.D. It is also the story of the Spanish explorers who came to the South as emissaries of a world that was on the threshold of modernity. The Spanish explorers were knights and adventurers, not planters or entrepreneurs. They were more medieval than modern.

I hasten to add that the South as a geographical region did indeed exist in the sixteenth century. Its unique features of land, water, vegetation, and climate had shaped the lives of the Indians until the arrival of the Spanish explorers, just as they shaped the lives of the later European colonists.

The sixteenth-century South was there. History has simply failed to acknowledge it. The reasons for this are understandable. The bulk of historical information on this period comes from the accounts by the chroniclers of the Spanish expeditions, accounts which in one sense are exceedingly rich in detail but in another are so woefully sparse that it has been extremely difficult to pin the expeditions down on the landscape. Thus the Spanish accounts have made interesting tales, but in and of themselves they have not been enough to give us a comprehensive view of the sixteenth-century South.

But the problem has not only been a matter of evidence. The sixteenth-century South has also been lost from view because it fell between the cracks of academic specialization, a fracturing of knowledge which began about the middle of the nineteenth century and still continues apace today. In the early nineteenth century, the human sciences were not very far advanced, but they were still undivided. The division began in the late 1820s when history became a professional enterprise under the leadership of Leopold von Ranke and his famous seminar at the University of Berlin. Ranke wanted history to be a universal science of humanity (Stein 1973:60–62). But because historians were largely limited to written information from the past, many parts of humanity were excluded from their purview. Other scholars stepped in to claim the neglected territory. Historians wrote about European elites and their politics, while folklorists took as their subject matter the poor, the rural, and the provincial. It was then left to sociologists to study contemporary conditions in European society, which was then in the throes of change brought on by the industrial revolution, and to speculate about and predict social forms and conditions that were yet to be (Abrams 1972).

The remaining pieces of humanity—the prehistoric and the preliterate—fell to anthropology. And the division of labor was not to end here. In the twentieth century anthropologists have, almost without exception, wanted to be members of the scientific fraternity. And following the well-known pattern of specialization in the natural sciences, anthropology began to fission in a remarkable way into a series of ethno-, socio-, archeo-, and paleospecialties. While this process of specialization led to advances in knowledge, it has also produced a diffuse sense of mission for anthropology as a whole. And it has led anthropologists to cast their findings in an esoteric terminology that isolates anthropological research from scholars in neighboring fields, particularly historians.

If an edifice of sixteenth-century southern history is to ever be built, it will require the labors of both historians and anthropologists. But as it stands now, these two scholarly trade unions are divided by differing senses of who they are and what they are doing, and to some extent they do not even speak the same language. Scholars who try to bridge the gap run the risk of being accused of deserting their own professions.

This state of affairs does not need to continue. There is already in existence a framework of ideas through which the history of the sixteenth-century South can be apprehended. It is a paradigm of historical theory and methodology developed by a group of French social historians who, in the early twentieth century, became dissatisfied with the highly specialized, positivistic researches of their colleagues. This historical paradigm began with the work of Marc Bloch and Lucien Febvre (Stoianovich 1976) and has continued in the work of such contemporary historians as François Furet, Georges Duby, Jacques Le Goff, Emmanuel Le Roy Ladurie, and, most particularly, Fernand Braudel. It is an approach to human action through time which satisfied the historian's requirement that the particulars of human action be reconstructed fully and exactly, while at the same time it satisfies the intellectual demands of economists, sociologists, and anthropologists who are particularly interested in discerning patterns, constraints, and causes in human society.

I do not wish to flog my reader with theory. But it may be helpful to set forth a brief summary of Braudel's (1980) conception of history. His central notion is that the time of social history is plural, with different aspects occurring on different time scales, and that the task of the historian or anthropologist is to sort out these various aspects and time scales and reconstruct them by appropriate means. The most obvious and familiar kind of historical phenomena are *events,* the stuff of history as it has traditionally been written. Events occur in the short term— within a few years, a year, or even within a day. Events are the stuff of everyday life, the subject of journals, newspapers, official and unofficial correspondence, and gossip. Events are easily accessible to consciousness. It is easy to think about events, and for this reason when scholars write about events they can present their accounts in a narrative form. A story can be told. Until quite recently, social historians have been inclined to denigrate this kind of history as being mere *"l'histoire événementielle"* (Darnton 1985).

In every human situation there are longer-term phenomena which go beyond short-term events. These devolve from the specific organization of the society in question. These longer-lasting phenomena include processes, cycles, and trends which may take, say, ten to fifty years to play themselves out. These are phenomena which may only be partly accessible to the consciousness of the people whose lives are shaped by them. Or they may be understood by some individuals who have a privileged perspective, but not by others. The nature of such phenomena varies from one kind of society to another and from one part of society to another. By this I mean such phenomena as the domestic cycle of kin groups, or the expansion and fissioning of unilineal descent groups, or the cyclical reorganization and corruption in traditional Chinese bureaucracy, or the cyclical rise and fall of prices in the modern European economic system.

Finally, there are social phenomena which occur over very long periods of time. It is in this realm that we deal with *structure;* that is, with phenomena and with relationships which place severe constraints on human action. Such phenomena may be wholly beyond the consciousness of people. They may endure for hundreds or even thousands of years. Structural phenomena include such matters as geography—the constraints imposed by landform, temperature, and rainfall or by avenues of trade and travel. They include technological constraints, such as hoe agriculture, or travel and transport by dugout canoe. They can include persistent social arrangements, such as matrilineal descent. They can even include persistent patterns of thought, such as the assumption that things exist in pairs of opposites, or the assumption that the macrocosm and the microcosm are structurally similar.

In any particular instance of the actions of individuals through time, the task of the scholar is to sort out the various kinds of time and to represent them in such a way that their interrelations are exposed. The real triumph of this approach to social history is its emphasis on the importance of structural phenomena of long duration. It is only by placing the smaller pieces of social history in relation to these long-term phenomena that they can be rendered fully intelligible. Braudel says it well: "In any case, it is in relation to these expanses of slow-moving history that the whole of history is to be rethought, as if on the basis of an infrastructure. All the stages, all the thousand explosions of historical time can be understood on the basis of these depths, this semistillness. Everything gravitates around it" (Braudel 1980:33). One advantage which this conceptual scheme offers to anthropologists is that it is a way out of the impasse created by the synchronic/diachronic dichotomy. This dichotomy works well enough for language because it is so self-contained and conservative. But it does not apply well to human societies.

As soon as one proceeds from the time of historical events to the time of social trends, cycles, or, even more, structural phenomena, one must resort to constructing theoretical models. Braudel's conception of models is consistent with his conception of social time; that is, one must construct models of phenomena of various durations. In a brilliant metaphor, he compares such models to ships.

> What interests me, once the boat is built, is to put it in the water to see if it will float, and then to make it ascend and descend the waters of time, at my will. The significant moment is when it can keep afloat no longer, and sinks . . . It seems to me that research is a question of endlessly proceeding from the social reality to the model, and then back again, and so on,

in a series of readjustments and patiently renewed trips. In this way the model is, in turn, an attempt at an explanation of the structure, and an instrument of control and comparison, able to verify the solidity and the very life of a given structure. (Braudel 1980:45)

Thus, one might, for example, construct a model of protohistoric southeastern Indian demography. One could then sail this demographic ship up and down the river of time. Presumably, it would hit the rocks as soon as one got upstream beyond the time when corn became a staple, and sailing in the other direction it would again hit the rocks at the time when epidemic diseases from the Old World were introduced. Structural changes occurred in both instances.

It now remains to show how this approach to social history, which largely developed out of the efforts of French social historians to understand European history, can help us understand the sixteenth-century Southeast. It is, I think, incontestable that the most important historical occurrence in the sixteenth-century South was the Hernando de Soto expedition. No other effort by Europeans of the time touched as many Indians as did this expedition. And no other corpus of sixteenth-century manuscripts covers as much of the Southeast. But where, exactly, did de Soto and his men go? How can we situate the events of this expedition on a map? The most authoritative reconstruction of the route is that of the U.S. De Soto Commission. This commission was organized to prepare information for the 400th anniversary of the expedition, and its report was published in 1939 (Swanton 1939). But scholars began doubting the accuracy of the U.S. De Soto Commission route almost before it was published, and as the years have gone by ever more insistent and serious doubts have been raised.

With more daring than good sense, I organized a seminar at the University of Georgia in 1979 whose purpose was to begin the task of establishing once and for all where de Soto went. The principals in this seminar were myself, Chester DePratter, and Marvin Smith. As the seminar proceeded, I quickly realized that by themselves the de Soto documents were not sufficiently detailed to allow the route to be reconstructed. This was so even with the help of the impressive amount of archeological research done on the South since the time the De Soto Commission did its work.

Our breakthrough came from an unexpected quarter. DePratter had obtained from the North Carolina Department of Archives a copy and a

translation of a remarkable document written by one Juan de la Bandera. Bandera was notary for Juan Pardo's expedition from coastal
South Carolina into the interior in 1567–68. Bandera was a superbly
compulsive notary who kept a day-by-day record of Pardo's expedition, noting down the names of most of the chiefs with whom Pardo
dealt. He often kept track of the number of leagues they traveled in a
day and he occasionally made observations on the changing character
of the country. In all, he gave much more detailed information than
was given by any of the de Soto chroniclers. Bandera's record of the
expedition was full enough that we were able to locate Pardo's movements on the landscape with reasonable confidence (DePratter, Hudson, and Smith 1983).

   Pardo visited five of the same Indian towns which de Soto had visited twenty-seven years earlier (Figure 1). Once we established the
locations of these towns, we had what no previous de Soto scholar
possessed—interior points of reference. This done, we then reexamined the de Soto documents and found that we could reconstruct de
Soto's route from Apalachee—in the vicinity of Tallahassee, Florida—
all the way to Chiaha in the Tennessee Valley (Hudson, Smith,
and DePratter 1984:65–77). Then we turned to the route beyond
Chiaha and we succeeded in reconstructing it to Mabila, in central
Alabama (DePratter, Hudson, and Smith 1985). In all these reconstructions there are some locations which will remain uncertain until
further archeological research is done, but we are reasonably confident
of the general route. We have continued taking the route west through
Mississippi, Arkansas, Oklahoma, and Texas in work that has yet to be
completed. And building upon this same foundation we have been able
to reconstruct the movements of Tristan de Luna's colonists in Alabama, Georgia, and Tennessee in 1559–1561 (Hudson, Smith, DePratter, and Kelley 1985).

   With this all too swift summary of our work, I have no doubt made
our task appear easier than it has been. In fact, it has taken us about
five years of fairly intensive work to accomplish what I have summarized, and more work is yet to be done. To most anthropologists, this
phase of our research must seem pedestrian, and our determination to
locate the route as precisely as possible must seem obsessive. Historians are far more likely to understand both the importance and the

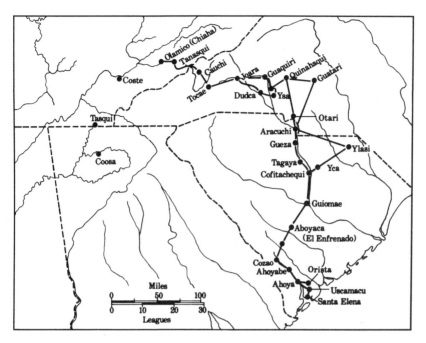

Figure 1
Juan Pardo's Expedition from Santa Elena to Chiaha.

difficulty of reconstructing a sequence of events from documents that are too few and so lacking in precision and completeness. Historians would also understand how the Pardo expedition helped us to reconstruct the de Soto expedition and how this in turn will help us to reconstruct the Luna expedition. The detailed reconstruction of events in the past can ramify in surprising ways. The light of understanding does not always come from the theoretical heavens—it can also come from the earth below.

So much for the expeditions as events. The next question is, what does the reconstruction of these routes of exploration tell us about long-term structural features in the protohistoric Southeast? I contend that it is only by reference to certain structural features that one can explain why Pardo and de Soto followed the routes they did. Pardo set out from Santa Elena, near present Beaufort, South Carolina, with instructions to discover a road to Zacatecas, where Spain possessed fabulously rich silver mines. But instead of proceeding westward, where he knew Zacatecas lay, Pardo headed north and northeast, going hundreds of miles out of his way before he turned west. Why did he do this? In part he did so because whatever their objectives might be, the sixteenth-century Spanish explorers had to go where they could find food. Since they were unable to supply themselves with food on their travels, they had to go to Indian centers of population where they could expropriate stores of corn, and centers of Indian population lay only in certain places.

This explains why Pardo went north and northeast from Santa Elena, and it explains why de Soto went out of his way to cross and recross the Flint River, which was wide and deep and presented great hazards, even though he could have gone directly northward without having gone near the Flint River. But he had to have the corn that was to be found at Capachequi (Figure 2), a small chiefdom that lay along Chickasawhatchee Creek to the southwest of present Albany, Georgia (Hudson, Smith, and DePratter 1984). Neither Pardo nor de Soto were stumbling blindly through the wilderness. They had Indians to guide them where they needed to go.

It has been known for quite some time that the southeastern chiefdoms specialized in the farming of favored soils, particularly the sandy alluvial soils which lay along the margins of rivers and creeks. However, this concentration of favored soils was a necessary but not a sufficient determinant of occupation. Not all suitable areas of sandy alluvial soils were the seats of chiefdoms in the sixteenth century. For example, when de Soto traveled from the chiefdom of Ocute on the Oconee River in Georgia to Cofitachequi on the Wateree River in South Carolina, he crossed a deserted area of over 130 miles. There were several areas of sandy, alluvial soil in this "desert," most particularly along the Savannah River. A century or so earlier, this part of the Savannah River was heavily occupied by Mississippian farmers, but in 1540 it was vacant. The reasons why it was abandoned are not yet clear, but it may ultimately be explainable in terms of the structure and organization of protohistoric chiefdoms. It is clear enough already that Mississippian centers of power did not last forever. They rose and fell, either because of some inner dynamic or inherent instability (DePratter 1983) or else because of competition with each other.

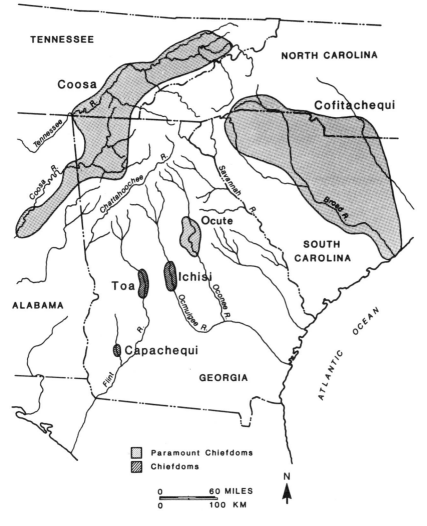

Figure 2
Some Sixteenth-Century Southeastern Chiefdoms.

The remarkable zigzagging path the de Soto expedition followed west of the Mississippi River gives us a vivid picture of a formidable structural barrier (Hudson 1984).[4] De Soto spent two of the four years of the expedition making repeated attempts to go westward from the Mississippi River, always hitting a veritable environmental wall and being forced to turn back. This barrier first showed up when de Soto sent a small party from Pacaha, on the western bank of the Mississippi River near Lake Wapanocca or Pecan Point, to explore toward the northwest (Figure 3). After traveling for several days in northern Arkansas, they finally came to a small village of hunters who told them that further north there were many buffalo and very few people. With this news the exploring party returned to Pacaha.

The barrier next appeared as the entire expedition traveled from the lower St. Francis River toward the northwest. They came to Coligua, near Batesville, Arkansas, on the White River, but here the Indians told them if they went further north they would come to a cold country where there were many buffalo and few people. From there they turned southward to the Arkansas River and again tried to go west, ascending the Arkansas River to about present Russellville, where the Indians told them that if they continued in that direction they would come to an uninhabited country of sandy wastes. They returned to the Mississippi, looping south and then east through the Ouachita Mountains. In the spring of 1540, near the mouth of the Arkansas River, de Soto died. The expedition, now under the command of Luis de Moscoso, again tried to go west, this time *south*west in an attempt to return to New Spain. In fact, they wanted to go west, but the necessity of getting food from the Indians forced them to go south. But they got no farther than about the Trinity River in Texas, where the land became so poor and the Indian populations so sparse that they realized they would starve to death if they continued. Once again they had to turn around and return to the Mississippi River. They spent their last winter building brigantines in which they escaped down the river the following summer, returning to New Spain by water.

In large part, this western barrier was demarcated by the rapid decline in rainfall that sets the West off from the East. But there may also have been additional environmental and social features of which we have as yet no clear understanding.

In many ways it is easier to discern the long and the short of histor-

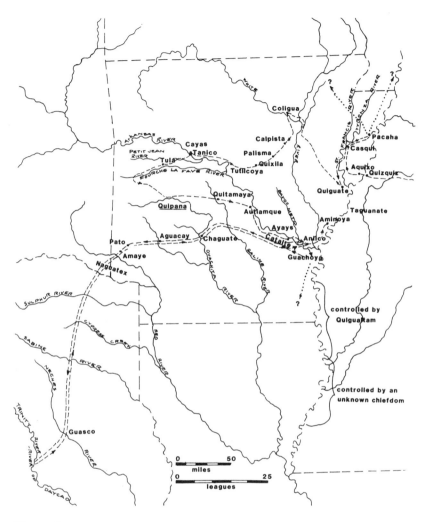

Figure 3
A Preliminary Map of the Route of the de Soto Expedition West of the
Mississippi River.

ical time in the sixteenth-century Southeast than it is to discern the
social and economic patterns of the middle range. In part, this is because the documentary record is so episodic. This makes it difficult to
follow social phenomena of any duration. But some patterns are clear
enough to at least begin making an interpretation.

It is possible, for example, to begin to describe the more important
organizational features of protohistoric political organization. From the
Juan Pardo expedition it is clear that there were three positions of political leadership in the protohistoric Southeast. These were *orata,* apparently a village headman; *mico,* a chief to whom several *oratas* were
subsidiary; and "paramount chief," a position for which Bandera unfortunately gives no Indian term. Pardo met with about eighty *oratas,*
he met with three *micos,* and he heard about the paramount chief of
Coosa, though the Indians forced him to turn back before he reached
Coosa, so he did not actually meet this man.

At the time of the de Soto expedition it is clear that Cofitachequi was
a paramount chiefdom, but when de Soto reached the main town of this
chiefdom he found that it was already beginning to decline because of
pestilence, evidently European in origin. By the time of the Pardo expeditions the decline of Cofitachequi had gone very far indeed. Not
only was there no paramount chief of Cofitachequi, there was not even
a *mico*—only an *orata.* However, Cofitachequi was still located at the
center of a remarkable convergence of trails, so that very many Indian
chiefs were gathered there to meet with Pardo. By constructing a so-
ciogram of the Indians who met with Pardo at Cofitachequi and elsewhere I have been able to reconstruct something of the constituency of
the chiefdom of Cofitachequi. It was quite large in extent, perhaps
stretching from the vicinity of the mouth of the Santee River and
Winyaw Bay on the Atlantic Coast northward up the Catawba-Wateree-Santee River to the mountains. Also, Cofitachequi controlled not
only the Catawba-Wateree-Santee River, but also the Peedee River up
to the narrows of the Yadkin.

If this reconstruction of the paramount chiefdom of Cofitachequi is
accurate, the chiefdom contained within itself considerable linguistic
diversity. The main towns were Muskogean-speaking, but other towns
were Catawban-speaking, and it is possible that still others spoke languages related to Yuchi and Cherokee (Rankin, Hudson, and Booker
1984).

Juan Pardo did not visit the paramount chief of Coosa, but Hernando de Soto did. The chiefdom of Coosa was one of the most powerful chiefdoms in the protohistoric Southeast. De Soto was told of the existence of Coosa when he reached Ocute and again when he reached Cofitachequi. But he did not reach a town that was subject to Coosa until he crossed the Blue Ridge Mountains and came to the island town of Chiaha in the French Broad River near present Dandridge, Tennessee. Like Cofitachequi, Coosa was surprisingly large in extent. After departing from Chiaha, de Soto traveled for twelve days through territory under the sway of Coosa until he reached the main town near present Carters, Georgia. And when he departed from the main town he traveled toward the southwest for an additional twelve days before he reached the southern limit of Coosa at the town of Talisi, near present Childersburg, Alabama (Hudson, Smith, Hally, Polhemus, and DePratter 1985).

Like Cofitachequi, Coosa was linguistically heterogeneous, though the heterogeneity appears to not have been as great as in Cofitachequi. The language of the main town of Coosa as well as of towns to the south appears to have been eastern Muskogean, while the languages spoken from about the Hiwassee River northward to Chiaha appear to have been Koasati.[5]

We are fortunate that the chiefdom of Coosa received yet another group of uninvited Spaniards. In 1560 a party of soldiers from the Tristan de Luna expedition made their way northward to Coosa (Hudson, Smith, DePratter, and Kelley 1985). Some in the party had been with de Soto. They found that Coosa had declined from what it had been at the time of the de Soto expedition. From incidents which occurred during this second visit, a number of valuable insights can be had into the organization of Coosa.

The most notable of these incidents was when the chief of Coosa persuaded Luna's men to send a contingent of soldiers along with some of his own warriors to wage a punitive attack on the Napochies, a tributary group on the Tennessee River which had been refusing to pay tribute to Coosa (Figure 4). What this means is that Coosa, and probably other paramount chiefdoms, had as their economic basis not merely redistribution but *tribute* as well. If it had been simply redistribution, nonpayment would not have led to reprisals. If this incident is at all representative, it means that within Coosa there were pronounced

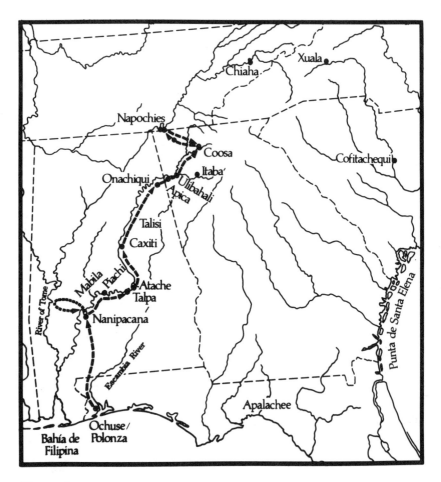

Figure 4
The Tristan de Luna Expedition.

fissive tendencies. The Napochies had broken away or were attempting to break away from the domination of Coosa. Luna's soldiers found Coosa scalps hanging from a pole in the plaza at one of their towns. This kind of conflict must have been common as late prehistoric Mississippian centers rose and declined in political importance.

This incident may also imply that Coosa was expansionist, that it was endeavoring to extend the territory of its political power by military means. Military conflict and perhaps military expansion were also implied by the fact that the northern towns of Coosa were heavily fortified.

In addition to these large paramount chiefdoms, there were also small chiefdoms in the Southeast which apparently had only two levels of command and which, so far as the documents reveal, were subsidiary to no paramount chief. It would seem that such was the case with most of the small chiefdoms of Toa and Ichisi in southern and central Georgia.

In the central Mississippi valley de Soto encountered powerful chiefdoms which were, if not larger in scale than Coosa and Cofitachequi, qualitatively different from them. In the record of de Soto's dealings with the chief of Casqui and the paramount chief of Pacaha, one gets the impression that these were men who were used to greater political complexity and subtlety than were the chiefs he had met before.

Although I have been concerned with the sixteenth-century South, the approach I am advocating can be applied much more broadly. In fact, I am convinced that as we continue to explore the sixteenth-century South we shall find strong research trails which lead to other times and other places. Marvin Smith has already begun to follow one of these trails. He became interested in a structural crisis I mentioned earlier—the rocks on which the ship of protohistoric Indian demography was torn asunder and sunk. He has pieced together archeological evidence of a sharp demographic decline in Georgia and Alabama during the decades just after the Spanish exploration (Smith 1984).

Smith's work leads directly to the Indians of the seventeenth-century South (1568–1670), a period in which evidence is even harder to come by than for the sixteenth century. Vast changes occurred among Indian societies in the seventeenth century, but there were no European observers on hand to write about them. Hence, the evidence is almost exclusively archeological. It is not going to be easy for archeologists to elucidate this important chapter of southeastern Indian social history.

In my opinion, the only direct avenue to understanding the southeastern Indians in the seventeenth century is to conduct long-term, detailed research in the areas occupied by the protohistoric chiefdoms. Mark Williams has begun such a study of the Oconee River, where the chiefdom of Ocute was located, and Leland Ferguson and Chester DePratter have begun a similar project in the Wateree River Valley, where the center of the grand chiefdom of Cofitachequi was located. The only other avenue is indirect; that is, to compare the sixteenth-century Southeast with the early eighteenth-century Southeast and to then infer what happened between these two periods of time.

The relatively obscure seventeenth century was brought to an end by yet another structural change. This was when France and England began their struggle for colonial supremacy in the South. During the next century, the eighteenth (1670–1781), the social history of the southeastern Indians cannot be understood apart from their participation in the modern world economy and in these international colonial struggles (Hudson 1981, 1984).

Southern anthropologists are in a position to play a significant role in adding an entire century to southern history and, in fact, to the history of North America. Moreover, they can do so in a way that is not theoretically trivial. Whether the final product is called anthropology or social history matters very little. The condition of knowledge in the human and social sciences in contemporary America is not so different from the condition of historical knowledge when Marc Bloch and Lucien Febvre embarked on their program of developing a new kind of social history. And southern anthropologists should take comfort and encouragement from the fact that Bloch and Febvre first launched their program from the University of Strasbourg, an institution that was no more in the mainstream of academia than are most southern universities today.

NOTES

1. I am grateful to the Center for the History of the American Indian at the Newberry Library for a fellowship in 1977–78, a gloriously unencumbered

year in which I was free to begin developing some of the ideas in this paper. This is the third incarnation of this paper. I first broached the subject in a paper entitled "The Crucial Problem in the Early History of the Southeastern Indians" at the 1978 Southern Anthropological Society meeting. I presented a derivative but far different paper, "An Unknown South: The World of Sixteenth-Century Indians," at the 1980 Chancellor's Symposium at the University of Mississippi. In each successive incarnation the paper has, I trust, become less programmatic and more substantive.

2. For a variety of reasons, the seventeenth century has received less attention from historians than it deserves. See Jack P. Green, Adapting to the New World, *Times Literary Supplement,* October 31, 1980, p. 1237.

3. The term "sixteenth-century South" has hardly been used. I searched the *Journal of Southern History* and found next to nothing. The one exception appears to be Carl Sauer's *Sixteenth Century North America* (Berkeley: University of California Press, 1971), a book which, as its title indicates, is not limited to the South.

4. This reconstruction of de Soto's route through Arkansas is subject to revision. In reconstructing this present version I have received invaluable assistance from members of the Arkansas Archeological Survey. I am particularly grateful to Hester Davis, Ann Early, John House, Dan Morse, and Frank Schambach and also to Michael Hoffman of the University of Arkansas Museum.

5. Apparently, this area of Koasati speakers coincides with the area in which the Dallas archeological phase occurs.

REFERENCES

Abrams, Philip, 1972. The Sense of the Past and the Origins of Sociology. *Past and Present* 55:18–32.

Bannon, John Francis, 1974. *The Spanish Borderlands Frontier, 1513–1821* (Albuquerque: University of New Mexico Press).

Braudel, Fernand, 1980. History and Social Sciences: The *Longue Durée.* In *On History,* Fernand Braudel (Chicago: University of Chicago Press), pp. 25–54.

Darnton, Robert, 1985. Revolution sans Revolutionaries. *New York Review of Books* 32:21–23.

DePratter, Chester B., 1983. Late Prehistoric and Early Historic Chiefdoms in the Southeastern United States. Ph.D. dissertation, University of Georgia.

DePratter, B., Charles M. Hudson, and Marvin Smith, 1983. The Route of

Juan Pardo's Explorations in the Interior Southeast, 1566–1568. *Florida Historical Quarterly* 62:125–128.

———, 1985. The Hernando de Soto Expedition: From Chiaha to Mabila. In *Alabama and the Borderlands: From Prehistory to Statehood,* Lawrence A. Clayton and Reid R. Badger, eds. (Tuscaloosa: University of Alabama Press).

Hudson, Charles, 1981. Why the Southeastern Indians Slaughtered Deer. In *Indians, Animals, and the Fur Trade: A Critique of Keepers of the Game,* Shepard Krech, ed. (Athens: University of Georgia Press), pp. 157–176.

———, 1984. The Genesis of Georgia's Indians. In *Forty Years of Diversity: Essays on Colonial Georgia,* Harvey H. Jackson and Phinizy Spalding, eds. (Athens: University of Georgia Press), pp. 25–45.

———, 1985. DeSoto in Arkansas: A Brief Synopsis. *Field Notes: Newsletter of the Arkansas Archeological Society* 205:3–12.

Hudson, Charles, Marvin Smith, David Hally, Richard Polhemus, and Chester DePratter, 1985. Coosa: A Chiefdom in the Sixteenth-Century Southeastern United States. *American Antiquity* 50:723–737.

Hudson, Charles, Marvin T. Smith, and Chester B. DePratter, 1984. The Hernando de Soto Expedition: From Apalachee to Chiaha. *Southeastern Archaeology* 3:65–77.

Hudson, Charles, Marvin Smith, Chester DePratter, and Emilia Kelley, 1985. The Tristan de Luna Expedition, 1559–1561 (paper presented at the Southeastern Archaeological Conference, Birmingham, Alabama).

Rankin, Robert, Charles Hudson, and Karen Booker, 1984. Linguistic Affiliation of Juan Pardo Expedition Place Names (paper presented at the 1984 American Anthropological Association Meeting).

Smith, Marvin T., 1984. Depopulation and Culture Change in the Early Historic Period Interior Southeast. Ph.D. dissertation, University of Florida.

Stein, Fritz, ed., 1973. *The Varieties of History: From Voltaire to the Present* (New York: Vintage Books).

Stoianovich, Traian, 1976. *French Historical Method: The Annales Paradigm* (Ithaca: Cornell University Press).

Swanton, John R., comp., 1939. *Final Report of the United States De Soto Expedition Commission.* House Document 71, 76th Congress, 1st session (Washington, D.C.: U.S. Government Printing Office).

Reordering Their World:
A Caddoan Ethnohistory

George Sabo III

In this paper I use English translations of early Spanish and French accounts to explore the conceptual world of Caddoan Indians at the time of contact and to determine how this world—and hence Caddoan culture—was altered as a result of interaction with Europeans.[1] Caddoan Indians living in the area now comprising eastern Texas, southwestern Arkansas, and northwestern Louisiana played a pivotal role in seventeenth- and eighteenth-century contests between Spain and France for control of the Trans-Mississippi South. By favoring opportunities for trade offered by the French over Spanish attempts at religious conversion, Caddoan responses to the events of this era strongly affected the extent to which European aims ultimately were achieved. Caddoan culture was also profoundly transformed in the struggle for supremacy between European competitors. Three primary questions are addressed in this study: (1) What cultural perceptions (or cultural categories) regarding persons, beings, and society existed among the Caddoan prior to contact? (2) How did these perceptions influence initial Caddoan responses to Europeans? (3) In what ways were these perceptions and the responses they engendered modified as a result of interaction with Europeans?

This attempt to examine historical events anthropologically, from "the native point of view," is certainly not unprecedented in studies of North American Indians (see Lewis 1942; Holder 1967; Martin 1978). Excellent treatments of Caddoan contact history also exist (Bolton 1915; Glover 1935; Griffith 1954; Newcomb 1961; John 1975), but these have been written from the western cultural perspective. My purpose is to reexamine historical events from another perspective.

APPROACH

My approach to the study of Caddoan contact history consists of two parts. The first part entails identification of the basic categories, structures, and themes of Caddoan culture—particularly concerning notions of persons, beings, and the organization of society—which existed at the time of European contact. Since ethnographic compilations (Swanton 1942; Griffith 1954; Newcomb 1961) lack detailed information on these subjects, it is necessary to determine what these categories were through reexamination of primary source materials. For this study I examine accounts of Caddoan ceremonialism and, using elements of symbolic/structuralist approaches to analysis (Leach 1967; Turner 1967; Geertz 1973; Boon 1982), I arrive at interpretations of what these cultural categories and relationships were. In relying for this initial part of the study on descriptions of ceremonies dating to the initial decades of contact between the Caddoan and Europeans, I am assuming that these descriptions accurately portray Caddoan culture at the time of contact.

The second part of this study focuses on specific examples of interaction between the Caddoan Indians and the Spanish and French prior to the transfer of the Louisiana Territory to the United States in 1803. Greeting ceremonies involving the formal reception of certain Europeans by the Caddoan on important occasions of contact are examined in detail. There is a practical as well as a theoretical justification for this focus. Practically, many of the key meetings between important Caddoan and European leaders were noted and described by early European chroniclers, whereas the routine, day-to-day interactions which typically followed were not. Theoretically, these occasions also provide a context for the kind of ritualized behavior in which cultural categories and perceptions play a prominent and, therefore, discernible role. The analytic orientation of this latter examination is based on Sahlins' work in *Historical Metaphors and Mythical Realities* (Sahlins 1981). Briefly, Sahlins' approach begins with the notion that the history of a people is organized by structures of significance derived from their culture. Thus, the events of history are ordered by culture, but also, in the process, culture may itself be reordered. Sahlins asks, how does the reproduction of a structure become its transformation?

The method of Sahlins' approach which I attempt to follow starts with an examination of the interaction between cultural categories and perceptions and the events and situations of the historic moment. It is precisely this interaction between cultural system and historic event that Sahlins attempts to understand, through structural analysis, as meaningful process. To achieve this understanding Sahlins examines in detail the interplay between cultural categories and perceptions and what he calls "structures of the conjuncture": relationships developed in the context of historic events which define the roles of participants and the nature of their interaction. Cultural categories and perceptions thus interact with historic events and situations through the actions of participating actors, all of whom have specifically constituted interests. When the situations encountered in practice depart from culturally derived expectations, the perceptions underlying these expectations may be altered. This results in a new, or "received," cultural category, modified from its prior form. As received cultural categories interact with events of subsequent historic moments, a dialectic is set into motion which over time may result in pronounced structural transformation.

SYMBOLIC ANALYSIS OF CADDOAN CEREMONIALISM

The basic categories, structures, and themes of Caddoan culture at the time of contact with Europeans may be determined, at least in general outline, through analysis of certain ceremonies described in the accounts of early European chroniclers (Table 1). Although the historical veracity of these accounts is compromised, in general, by observer biases and other shortcomings, they do contain information on the *form* and *content* of Caddoan ceremonialism in reasonably accurate detail. By *form* I refer to specific ceremonial acts along with the sequence of their performance, identification of actors, the physical and temporal setting of the performance, and the material paraphernalia used in a ceremony. By *content* I refer to cultural categories, themes, and values which may be symbolized by the formal aspects of a ceremony. Whereas the form of a ceremony may be determined observationally or read from texts, the content must either be elicited from informants or interpreted. Since in this study I am working with histor-

Table 1
Documentary Sources of Ethnographic Data on Early Historic
Caddoan Ceremonialism

Date	Chronicler	Reference	Ceremonial Descriptions
1687	Joutel	Joutel 1966	Greeting ceremony, first fruits ceremony, food blessing, privilege of seating, calumet ceremony
1687	Douay	Shea 1852	Greeting ceremony, note on ceremonial dress
1688–89	Massanet	Casis 1899	Food blessing
1690	De Tonti	Falconer 1975	Washing before entering fire temple
1690–91	Casanas	Hatcher 1927	Giving thanks with pipe, food blessing, privilege of seating, Gran Xinesi communicating with Supreme Being through two children, belief in the afterlife, origin myth, ancestor feasts
1710–16	Hidalgo	Hatcher 1927	First fruits ceremony
1712	Penicault	French 1869	Calumet ceremony, bloodletting
1710–18	Espinosa	Hatcher 1927	Calumet ceremony, origin myth, perpetual fire, house of the little children, offerings to the fire, souls of the dead, forecasting ceremony, first fruits ceremony, planting ceremony, making hoes, after-harvest ceremony
1716	Ramon	Foik 1933	Calumet ceremony
1718–19	Celiz	Hoffman 1935	Calumet ceremony, house-building ceremony
1719	La Harpe	Smith 1958–59	Calumet ceremony
1721	Morfi	Morfi 1932	Calumet ceremony, origin myth, perpetual fire, house of the little children, offerings to the fire, forecasting ceremony, first fruits ceremony, planting ceremony, after-harvest ceremony

ical texts, the cultural significance of Caddoan ceremonies—their content—must be interpreted.

Evaluation of Caddoan ceremonies in terms of scheduling, purpose, range of participants, and nature of the ritual activities indicates that a four-part series comprised a singularly important ceremonial sequence. This sequence unfolded over a major portion of the year and centered upon insuring the successful production of food resources. The forecasting ceremony was held in February and was followed by an early spring planting ceremony and a summer first fruits ceremony. The sequence concluded in September with the after-harvest ceremony which, in the eyes of European observers, was the single most important ceremonial occasion of the Caddoan year. Caddoan food production, it is important to note, was as much a social matter as it was economic. Caddoan social categories therefore played an important role in the organization of food-producing activities. Furthermore, since Caddoan social categories were cosmogonically derived and therefore imbued with ritual significance (as discussed in greater detail below), one implication of these relationships is that the economic, social, and ritual aspects of Caddoan food production were based on a common set of structuring principles. Comprising what we may safely regard as the paramount set of ritual activities among early historic Caddoan groups, this ceremonial sequence should provide fertile ground for the analysis of aboriginal symbolism and interpretation of its cultural significance.

The elite participants of the four ceremonies, variously referred to as priests, elders, doctors, medicine men, old men, chiefs, or conjurers, typically engaged in one or more purification rituals prior to the main ceremonial events. One ritual involved the consumption of a ceremonial tea brewed from laurel leaves. Another purification rite involved smoking tobacco in pipes that were passed among the elite practitioners. By convention the exhaled smoke was blown toward the sky, toward the earth, and toward the four cardinal directions, symbolic of the three primary dimensions of the cosmos. Both of these ritual acts—drinking tea and smoking tobacco—had the effect of transforming the ritual practitioners from a secular state of being to a sacred state of being necessary for their intercessory role of communicating with the Supreme Being on behalf of the Caddoan people. Offering tobacco to the fire, sometimes as an additional preparatory ritual, similarly established through symbolic means the sanctity of the ceremonial context in which the Supreme Being was to be petitioned.

We may turn now to the symbolism specifically associated with the four ceremonies comprising the Caddoan ceremonial sequence. In the forecasting ceremony, the elite ritual practitioners gathered in the fire temple and first drank ceremonial tea. Then with their faces turned toward the wall they prayed to the Supreme Being. Facing the wall as opposed to facing the fire—the symbol of the Supreme Being on earth—seems to be an explicit positional representation of the inability of the ritual participants to communicate directly with the Supreme Being. While this interpretation might by itself seem arbitrary, it is consistent with another major symbolic element of this ceremony which involved the use of a carefully preserved and decorated feather to represent an eagle flying toward the heavens to communicate with the Supreme Being. Only after these acts are the elite practitioners able to "make their almanacs" which they then relate to the rest of the people who have assembled outside of the fire temple.

In the planting ceremony preceding the actual preparation of the fields, all of the women, including young girls, gathered together to make two or three mats woven of fine strips of cane provided by an older woman who also acted as supervisor. These mats were turned over to the village captain, who made an offering of the mats in the fire temple in order that the people might have good crops during the coming year. The symbolic function of the mats in this ritual context represented the productive efforts of women, who were primarily responsible for tending the fields as the crops matured. The use of mats to symbolize the productive efforts of women is appropriate in this context since mats are a major element of Caddoan material culture, used for many purposes both secular and sacred, and they are, of course, made by women.

Descriptions of the first fruits ceremonies differ to some extent in detail but otherwise seem consistent with regard to the identification of primary symbols. Upon maturation of a new crop, the first fruits ceremony was performed throughout the community at individual households. Evidently the elaborateness of the ceremony depended upon the wealth of the particular household. Very wealthy individuals, for example, might invite the entire village to the ceremony and an accompanying feast, while less wealthy individuals might invite only a few guests and poor households would invite no guests at all. In any case, a portion of the new crop was gathered and first prepared by some form of cooking to symbolically transform the substance from "plant" status to "food" status. This seems to be structurally analogous to the secular to sacred transformation of human participants in ritual contexts. Joutel (1966), for example, observed that roasted ears of corn were first placed in a basket which then was set upon a ceremonial stool (otherwise reserved for the exclusive use of the *caddi,* or village leader). This act of elevating also symbolized the sacredness of the prepared food by reference to the dimensional and hierarchical categories of the cosmos. Next the food offering was blessed, and here again we encounter some variation in the separate descriptions of this act. Joutel mentions an elder stretching out his hands over the food and talking a long time; Casanas speaks of a *caddi* throwing a portion of the food into the fire, onto the ground, and to each side; and Espinosa refers to a "saint" or old man who mutters prayers and offers the fire a sacrifice of the food (Hatcher 1927). These versions according to which the food was blessed indicate the use of the symbolism of fire (representing life and creative force on earth) and of the dimensional categories of the cosmos to sanctify the food prior to its consumption.

The after-harvest ceremony, during which a large gathering of people assembled from all of the villages throughout the region, was the single most important ritual and festival occasion of the Caddoan year in terms of the number of participants, range of ritual activities, and density of symbolic associations. The primary symbols of this ceremony and their interpretations may be summarized as follows.

First, a special place was cleared for the ceremony at the fire temple of the main village. This cleaning was symbolically analogous to the practice of people washing themselves before entering the fire temple—an obvious act of ritual purification based on the structural oppositions of purity and pollution, sacred and profane. The elite ritual participants, after additional rites of purification, sent young men out to hunt deer for the coming feast. According to Morfi's (1932) account these men were sent out, day after day for six days, in the four cardinal directions. On the first night of the ceremony the participants were segregated, with elite practitioners inside the fire temple and the others gathering around fires outside. Here an inside versus outside dichotomy is used to symbolize the hierarchical categorization of these two classes of ritual participants. Inside the temple the elite practitioners were seated upon their ceremonial stools, which further symbolizes their superordinate status. The structural association of the upward direction of the heavens and the heavenly locus of supernatural powers legitimizes the authority of the elite participants to conduct sacred ceremony on behalf of the Caddoan people.

After midnight women from each household came in groups of three and offered gifts of food to the elite functionaries in the fire temple. Here the arrangement of women in groups of three symbolizes the three major dimensions of the cosmos (up toward heaven, down toward earth, and horizontally to the four cardinal directions). Meanwhile, an observer kept track of the movement of the constellation Pleiades, for when these stars were aligned perpendicular to the fire temple the ceremony shifted to the next phase of its unfolding. Since the Pleiades were referred to as "the women," it may be that this alignment symbolized fertility and propagation, which are the central themes of this ceremony. Support for this interpretation is found in a myth related by Casanas where the woman who assisted the original old men in the construction of the heavens still resides there, daily giving birth to the sun, the rain, the crops, and other periodic, life-giving elements of nature.

The next phase of the ceremony following the alignment of the stars began with two of the chief conjurers moving to an open area surrounded by a circle of green cane stalks, where they were seated in an elevated position upon their ceremonial stools. In this context the symbolism of the cosmic dimensions again sanctifies the authority of the conjurers to direct ritual activities which in this instance consist of leading a choir of women, assembled in ranks according to age grade, in sacred songs. Meanwhile, three other elders marched in procession from a nearby arbor. When the three elders reached the sacred circle of cane stalks the singing ceased and additional food offerings were made by each woman.

Singing resumed until dawn at which time the participants all greeted the sun with thanks for the year's crops and also beseeched the sun for aid in coming events. Foot races were held in which participants were grouped by sex and age, and then the people all danced in circular formation until their exhaustion finally brought the ceremony to an end.

The foregoing considerations of Caddoan ritual symbolism, though briefly presented and probably containing gaps owing to the incomplete nature of existing documentary accounts, does, I think, provide sufficient basis for the identification of some of the major cultural themes which rendered meaningful the Caddoan view of the universe. In this world view the human social order may clearly be seen as a subset of a larger cosmological order governing all beings, including supernaturals. This cosmological order was perceived in terms of complex, intersecting arrangements of categories and contrasts, dimensions and hierarchies. The cosmological order also possessed a sacred quality: it represented life and well-being. Disorder represented suffering and death. Disorder resulted when structural categories and relationships were not maintained. Conversely, disorder could be avoided or redressed through appropriate ritual which, in effect, brought into play supernatural powers to balance critical elements of the cosmos. Although such powers were attributed in varying degrees to many supernatural beings, clearly the most important and singularly powerful was Ayo-Caddi-Aymay, the "Captain of the Sky" or Supreme Being.

Caddoan society was organized congruently with the multilayered cosmological ordering of supernatural beings/powers. The paramount chief or *xinesi* stood at the apex of the hierarchically ordered Hasinai confederacy. He possessed considerable authority both in religious and in civil affairs, the boundaries of which were blurred. Tribal divisions within the confederacy each had a civil authority known as *caddi*, who were subordinate to the *xinesi*. Each *caddi* was assisted by several *canahas* in addition to other, lower-ranking village officials bearing the titles *chaya* and *tanma*. This group of community leaders seems to have functioned largely in the realm of civic duties (when such can be distinguished from purely religious ones) with responsibility for sacred matters resting with a class of shaman known as *conna* (Griffith 1954:58–68).

The Caddoan social order can be interpreted as a reproduction of the hierarchical ordering of beings and their associated powers as defined in Caddoan cosmology. This social order included a differential distribution of political decision-making power as well as religious authority to conduct sacred ritual, corresponding to hierarchical rank or position. Since human efforts on behalf of the maintenance of cosmological order were truly regarded as sacred affairs, the organization and structure of Caddoan society incorporated both secular and sacred statuses. Sacred activities, furthermore, necessitated a sanctified pose or state of being on the part of those high-status individuals who possessed the requisite authority to perform them.

CADDOAN CULTURE IN CONTACT AND TRANSFORMATION

A social order reproduced from cosmology, a notion of power corresponding to the hierarchical position ascribed to various beings (human and supernatural), and a concept of sacredness pervading many cultural institutions and formal practices are some of the culturally defined categories and perceptions Caddoan Indians brought to the contact situation. The extent to which this cultural system influenced early contacts can be assessed by considering the manner in which the Spanish and French were initially received by the Caddoan.

The period of regular and increasingly intensive contact in the midst of competing interests between Spain and France began in 1684 with the establishment of a small French outpost at Matagorda Bay founded by Robert Cavelier, Sieur de La Salle (Bolton 1912). Two years later La Salle and a small company of soldiers and priests briefly contacted the Hasinai during an abortive expedition to the Illinois territory. The following year, 1687, La Salle again departed his post at Matagorda Bay, this time with a larger party including Henri Joutel, Father Anastasius Douay, and La Salle's brother, who also was a priest. La Salle was murdered shortly thereafter but several members of the group pressed on and soon reached the Hasinai settlement they had visited the previous year. In his account of the expedition, Joutel (1966) describes how twelve elders marched out of the village to greet them, painted and dressed in their finest skins and decorated with belts, feathers, and assorted trade goods (undoubtedly obtained through trade with neighboring Indian groups in contact with Spanish settlements in Mexico). Bearing swords and clubs probably emblematic of their elite status, the elders were grouped in formation, flanked on either side by youths and warriors. Upon reaching the French the procession came to a halt, and raising up their right hands above their heads the elders cried out what must have been a salutation. The French were then embraced and the calumet of peace was smoked. This greeting was followed by exchanges of gifts and, later on in the village, feasts were held.

After a brief stay with the Hasinai, Joutel and his party continued on toward the northeast through Kadohadacho territory and four months later reached the nation of Cahaynohoua, possibly the Cahinnio Caddo. At this place another elaborate greeting ceremony took place. A company of elders attended by some young men and women came to Joutel's cottage bearing a calumet adorned with feathers and singing as loudly as they could. Entering the cottage, they continued singing as they took Cavelier the priest (La Salle's brother, whom they took to be the "chief" of the French party) by the arms and led him out to a specially prepared place where they laid a great handful of grass at his feet. Two others brought "fair water" in an earthen dish and washed his face, then sat him on a skin. The elders took their places around the priest and the leading elder stuck two wooden forks into the ground and laid a red-painted wooden stick across them. Over the sticks he draped two skins on which he then laid the pipe. All began to sing again, this time to the accompaniment of hollow gourds filled with gravel. One of the Indians sat behind Cavelier and rocked him in time to the music. When the song ended the leading elder brought two maidens, one carrying a sort of collar and the other an otter's skin, which they placed on the wooden forks at the ends of the pipe. Then the maidens sat on opposite sides of the priest, facing each other with their legs extended before them, and the leading elder laid Cavelier's legs across those of the two maidens. Meanwhile one of the elders tied a feather to the hair on the back of Cavelier's head. By this time the priest was greatly discomforted and asked the Indians to take him back to his cottage, which they did. However, the Indians stayed up all night singing, and in the morning fetched him again and resumed their ceremony. At this point the leading elder took the calumet and, filling it with tobacco and lighting it, he offered it to Cavelier only after advancing and drawing back six times. After everyone smoked, the pipe and sticks were wrapped in a skin case and were presented to the priest as a token of peace.

Comparable greeting ceremonies were also accorded the Spanish. Father Massanet and de Leon, the first Spaniards to directly contact the Hasinai in eastern Texas, were warmly welcomed in 1688 and were invited to reside among the Indians the following year (Casis 1899). Celiz (Hoffman 1935) relates the reception of Governor Alarcón upon his arrival at a Hasinai village during his inspection tour of 1718–19. Alarcón was taken down off his horse by the Indians and carried to a straw hut which had been made ready for him. Prior to entering, Alarcón's face and hands were washed and dried with a special cloth. Then he was carried into the house, two chiefs holding his shoulders, and he was seated upon a bench. The calumet of peace was then shared. Soon another house was built for Alarcón, on the completion of which the Indians staged another celebration. Dressed in gala outfits, the entire village assembled around a great bonfire lit in front of the house, near which a wooden bench was set and skins were laid out. The principal Indians and chiefs went inside the house and placed some white feathers on Alarcón's head and tied across his forehead a strip of black cloth. Leading him outside, the Indians seated Alarcón on the skins so he could lean back and be supported by one of the leading Indians who was seated on the bench. Accompanied by drums, the assembled Indians, who were arranged in groups according to their age and sex, began to sing. Four bonfires were lit and superintendents carrying burning torches in their hands kept the Indians in their ranks. From time to time the leader of the ceremony interrupted the singing to offer words of greeting to Alarcón and to welcome him to their village.

These examples of greeting ceremonies are replete with ritual and symbolism indicative of the sacredness in which these events were held. Especially important in this regard is the fact that prior to European contact the Caddoan scrupulously guarded their territories against intrusion, allowing traders from other Indian tribes access only to the periphery of their lands (John 1975:169). It is therefore evident from the elaborateness of the greeting ceremonies and the specialized treatment accorded certain individuals that these Europeans were regarded highly and, specifically, in terms of those qualities which defined the elite or superordinate categories of Caddoan social organization. So perceived, the Europeans were probably considered during this early period as being capable of manipulating sacred powers which might be exerted in the realm of cosmological affairs upon which Caddoan well-being was founded. This may well explain the enthusiastic acceptance of these first Europeans by the Caddoan. Conversely, many Caddoan cultural traits, including their well-defined social hierarchy based on hereditary succession, their belief in a single omnipotent deity, and their agricultural self-sufficiency, were very compatible with the Europeans' belief system. The fit between Caddoan and European cultural categories was probably a major factor underlying amicable early contacts.

While the Caddoan seem to have entertained both Spanish and French in a similar fashion, the respective aims of the Spanish and French were of markedly different form and purpose. The Spanish attempted to establish a system of missions and presidios throughout Caddoan territory which would be instrumental in religiously converting the Indians and gathering them into compact settlements (Bolton 1939). An additional outcome of this program anticipated by the Spanish was that Indian sentiments would be persuaded against any rivals of Spain (particularly the French), thereby establishing a native barrier to foreign encroachment (Griffith 1954:136). Two implications for the Indians of this potential relationship did, however, prove detrimental to Spanish objectives. First, acquiescence to the Spanish colonial system would require major changes in settlement and social organization that the Caddoan were simply unwilling to make at a single turn. Second, the Indians stood to gain little in the way of tangible material benefits through cooperation with the Spanish. Spanish colonial policy emphasized religious conversion over trade. This coupled with the high cost of transporting goods overland from centers of Spanish occupation to these distant outposts meant that the Spanish system could offer little beyond the hope for a greater reward in worlds to come in return for the major cultural sacrifices the Indians would have to make. Since Caddoan cosmology already included the belief that when the souls of the dead "are gathered together they will enter another world to live anew" (Hatcher 1927:294), the prospects of Spanish Catholicism were, for the Indians, certainly not extraordinary. This in addition to the disharmonious clash which would result upon any attempt to orchestrate Caddoan cosmology and Spanish aims of resettlement and consolidation rendered Spanish objectives, in the end, unreachable.

The Spanish missions established in eastern Texas in 1689 were withdrawn by 1693 as a result of these problems. In subsequent response to the establishment of a French trading post at Natchitoches in Louisiana Territory in 1713, the Spanish reasserted their presence in eastern Texas by 1715, and by 1721 there were six missions supported militarily by two presidios. But again due largely to the difficulty of supporting these far-flung outposts, this number was reduced by half in 1730. The continual failure of the Spanish to maintain an assertive presence among the Caddoans, coupled with Spanish missionizing objectives contrary to Caddoan perceptions of independence and self-sufficiency, must have certainly compromised the sacred/powerful associations initially attributed to the Spanish.

In contrast to this the French sought mainly to engage in trade with the Caddoan Indians. The French thus posed no immediate threat to Caddoan culture, offering instead an opportunity to acquire many useful and exotic goods in exchange for horses (which could be acquired in one way or another from the Spanish as well as from neighboring Indian tribes) and furs. The French trade system was therefore not only more compatible initially with the cultural categories and perceptions of the Caddoan, it also provided the basis for the larger set of economic relationships which developed subsequently between the Caddoan and both the French and Spanish. In retrospect, the end results of Caddoan response to European contact are clear: seemingly innocuous at first, submission to the French trade system set into motion a dependency-generating process by which the Indians came to rely increasingly upon the traders for a variety of goods upon which the very means of their existence had come to depend. The acquisition of horses and guns played a particularly crucial role in this dependency-generating process, for many scholars believe that these acquisitions were instrumental in shifting Caddoan subsistence from its precontact basis on agriculture to a subsequently greater reliance on hunting (see Griffith 1954:148–151). Changes in subsistence were not the only result of these economic relations with Europeans; many other aspects of Caddoan culture were modified. Possession of horses, for example, provided a new means for achieving social distinction available to members of all Caddoan social strata. The French trade system similarly made available to individuals of all social classes the many items they had come to require for satisfaction of personal and subsistence needs. By the end of the eighteenth century trade goods were widespread throughout Caddoan society. As subsistence pursuits shifted to greater reliance upon European technology (particularly horses and guns), it became less incumbent upon the Caddoan of lower statuses to beseech the supernatural for assistance through the religious elite. In short, trade with Europeans, and specifically the introduction of horses and European technology, served as a leveling mechanism by providing members of all Caddoan social strata access to positions of status independent of the traditional hereditary system. Subversion of the religious authority of the traditional elite would certainly seem to have been one outcome of these changes.

Support for this interpretation is provided by indications that by the late eighteenth century high-status positions were no longer based on the former categories of heredity and sacred power. De Solis, for example, remarked in 1768 that the Caddoan "esteem the men who are handsome, brave, and strong because they appoint the strongest and most valiant as captains" (Kress 1931:70). De Mézières also noted in 1777 that, with the exception of war parties, the Hasinai no longer recognized a paramount position of authority (Bolton 1914:2:166). While it would be unwise to place too much weight on these statements, they do suggest that Caddoan leadership positions had shifted from a sacred to a secular basis of authority by the end of the eighteenth century.

The broader implication of this cultural shift is that the sacred ritual program for maintaining cosmological order and balance—and thus ensuring well-being and the satisfaction of needs—was undermined and eventually replaced by secular concerns focused on maintaining trade relations with Europeans. If this was true we would expect to see the sacred pose transcending earlier relations between the Caddoan and Europeans replaced by later, more clearly secular concerns. This hypothesis can be tested by examining historical descriptions of Caddoan and European interaction during the latter half of the eighteenth century.

In 1752 the Spanish commandant Don Manuel Antonio de Soto Bermúdez traveled to eastern Texas in an attempt to counter growing French trade interests in the region (Hackett 1931–46:4:46ff.). Arriving at the village of the Nacogdoches (one of the Hasinai groups), Bermúdez presented the chief and his primary officers presents which the Indians gratefully accepted. The Nacogdoches chief in turn invited Spanish settlement in the village for purposes of trade, vowing to abstain from further trade with the French. Pushing on to Hasinai settlements closer to the French post at Natchitoches, Bermúdez was not so cordially received. The Nadote chief, believing that the Spanish intended to cut off all trade with the French, strongly objected and sent Bermúdez in quick retreat with threats against his life. The Nadote furthermore summoned their neighbors to similarly resist Spanish attempts to curtail the all-important trade relations with the French.

In 1767–68 Fray Gaspar José de Solís made an inspection tour of the east Texas missions during which he kept his observations in a daily diary. Included in his lengthy and detailed account are notes concerning his experiences with (as well as his impressions of) the Caddoan groups residing in the vicinity of the missions (Kress 1931:61–67). De Solís' account clearly indicates that encounters with Caddoan Indians were primarily characterized by exchanges of gifts: there is little indication of the elaborate ceremonialism witnessed a half-century earlier. On the contrary, animosity toward the Spanish seems to have developed, at least among some Caddoan groups. The perception of growing hostility was a focus of great concern among the Spanish upon their acquisition of Louisiana Territory in 1763. Relations between the Spanish and the Caddoan after that date developed in large measure as a result of attempts, by members of both groups, to reduce or at least control animosities which might interfere with other, pragmatic concerns.

Following acquisition of Louisiana Territory, Spain found it expedient to consolidate Caddoan support by maintaining elements of the old French trading system to which the Indians had grown accustomed. In this context Athanase de Mézières, well known among the Kadohadacho, Natchitoches, and Yatasis bands and related by marriage to the St. Denis family (who for decades had represented French interests in the Red River area), was appointed lieutenant governor of Natchitoches. One of the problems immediately facing de Mézières was a series of disturbances along the northern border of the Caddo area caused by groups of Comanche, Iscani, Kichae, Tonkawa, Taovaya, and Tawakoni—known collectively as Norteños or Nations of the North—who had been hostile to the Spanish and their Indian neighbors both in Texas and Louisiana. De Mézières chose to employ economic sanctions toward this end; namely, cutting off access by the Norteños to Spanish trade goods.

In the spring of 1770 de Mézières sought to consolidate support for his plan by gathering together at Natchitoches the leaders of the Kadohadacho, Natchitoches, and Yatasis bands with whom he felt he could place his trust. De Mézières regarded the support of the Caddoan as crucial to his objectives, since only by their observance of his sanctions could trade goods effectively be prevented from reaching the Norteños. Conversely, if the Norteños were eventually brought to peace, the Caddoans' own trade networks could accordingly be extended (Bolton 1914:1:140–142). With these thoughts in mind de Mézières honored the Kadohadacho and Yatasis headmen by presenting them with commemorative Spanish medals, and he attempted to impress upon the Caddoan the benefits they could realize through allegiance to Spain and by supporting his efforts to bring peace to the region. To further encourage their support de Mézières also promised to appoint traders to serve the Caddoan villages (Bolton 1914:1:142–143).

As a result of de Mézières' appeal the Kadohadacho medal chief Tinhiouen agreed to host a peace council in his village with the Norteños leaders. This meeting took place in October 1770, at which time de Mézières made it very plain to the Norteños that they must cease their hostilities and, if they did, allegiance to Spain could be an important step toward restoration of access to trade goods. Tinhiouen and the Yatasis medal chief Cocay followed with speeches in support of de Mézières. The Norteños headmen responded by pointing out that they had for some time been maintaining peace with neighboring Spanish settlements and would continue to do so. In return de Mézières promised to meet with them the following spring, at which time the establishment of trade relationships would be discussed (Bolton 1914:1:206–220).

De Mézières subsequently was unable to keep his promise to the Norteños due to the refusal of his superior, Governor Unzaga, to go along with this plan (Bolton 1914:1:232–233). However, the Hasinai chief Bigotes decided to meet with the Norteños in de Mézières' stead, and he subsequently traveled to Natchitoches carrying two buffalo skins which had been specially decorated to symbolize his mission. One skin was pure white to indicate that there should be no further bloodshed among the Indians; the other skin was decorated with four crosses representing the four Norteños groups who, at the previous council, had agreed to the peace treaty (John 1975:398).

De Mézières' Caddoan intermediaries had many reasons to support the conciliation between the Spanish and the Norteños. In addition to extending their own trade outlets, the Caddoan were attracted to the prospect of establishing a cordon of friendly Norteño villages which would provide an effective buffer between them and Apache, Comanche, and Osage groups to the north and west. For example, in 1773 Bigotes (by then known as Sauto) protested strongly to Governor Ripperda against removal of Spanish garrisons from several eastern Texas posts, fearing loss of protection from raids by the Apache (Bolton 1915:387). In this instance we see a Caddoan leader appealing to the Spanish authority to wield secular powers on behalf of the well-being of the Caddoan people.

The foregoing summary of selected events indicates that by 1770 and certainly thereafter Caddoan interaction with the Spanish was motivated by strong political and economic concerns which had developed in the context of trade relationships previously established with the French. Though aspects of traditional belief and symbolism continued to play a role in these proceedings (as best illustrated by Bigotes' use of decorated buffalo skins to publicly announce and sanctify his mission to the Norteños), the actions of Caddoan leaders on behalf of the well-being of their people are increasingly secular in their basis and in their effects. Political and economic measures dominate; sacred mediation clearly becomes secondary. One additional set of circumstances developed in this context may be cited in support of this conclusion. As a result of epidemics in the late 1770s several Caddoan villages were drastically reduced in population and many important leaders died. In many instances surviving Caddoan villages appealed to the Spanish authorities to appoint replacement chiefs. As John (1976:499) notes, these events bear fateful testimony to the disruptive effects of warfare and disease upon the orderly and hereditary succession to chiefly position the Caddoan formerly maintained. Certainly these effects played a major role in the breakdown of Caddoan social organization and the subversion of the traditional sacred power structure. But additionally, these examples of deference to Spanish authority illustrate a fundamental conceptual shift involving a replacement of belief in traditional supernatural beings/powers by belief in Europeans and their institutions as overseers of life's needs and, therefore, as the ultimate source of Caddoan well-being.

CONCLUSION

Structural change in Caddoan culture as a result of contact with Europeans was the product of a complex set of changing conceptual relationships. Prior to contact the Caddoan believed that their well-being depended on an ordered and balanced set of categories, statuses, and relationships among beings/powers populating a cosmogonically derived universe. Upon contact Europeans were perceived initially in terms of this system of beliefs. The accounts of Bermúdez, de Solís, and especially de Mézières indicate that, by the late eighteenth century, three important changes in these beliefs had taken place. First, Europeans were no longer accorded positions of sacred status in the minds of the Caddoan; they were dealt with, commonly, as principally secular beings when pragmatic concerns turned increasingly to an emphasis on European political and economic institutions. Second, status positions within Caddoan society underwent a shift from a sacred to a secular basis of authority, and the multitiered hierarchy of high-status positions was reduced to a fewer number of levels. Finally, Caddoan belief in cosmogonically derived, supernatural beings/powers was replaced by belief in nonsacred Europeans and their institutions as the main providers of means to satisfy life's needs and, therefore, as the ultimate sources of Caddoan well-being. By the late eighteenth century the Caddoan had little choice but to arrange their affairs within the context of overpowering European interests.

Left unanswered by these interpretations, however, is a central question: through what process of contact and interaction with Europeans did these structural changes within Caddoan culture occur? What deeper cultural transformations can be identified, and what fundamental categories or relationships did these changes serve to maintain?

Perhaps the most significant deep-level categorical shift mediating the structural changes noted above was the subversion of a rigidly hierarchical Caddoan authority structure which had been perceived on both cosmological and earthly planes. This status/power structure was not only secularized in the context of interaction with Europeans, but it was simplified and compressed as one result of the acquisition of European technology which permitted access to positions of status among a wider portion of the Caddoan populace. This mediating role of the principle of hierarchy provides an important clue with respect to the identification of deep-level processes involved in historic Caddoan culture change.

If we regard the hierarchy of status and power in Caddoan society as an important symbol in the wider system of cultural categories and relationships, an important shift in the meaning of this symbol can be identified which brought about other changes in the encompassing belief system. In traditional (or precontact) Caddoan belief, high social status and its attendant sacred power to intercede with the supernaturals on behalf of the Caddoan people was a symbol of the cosmogonically derived universe within which human wants and needs could be satisfied. The primary symbolic referent in this cosmology was the Supreme Being, Ayo-Caddi-Aymay, who was the embodiment of relationships between the Caddoan people and the means to sustain life and well-being on earth. Later this symbolism changed as Caddoan belief was redirected from a cosmological order to a pragmatic, political, and economic order upon which life and well-being subsequently came to depend. Accordingly, European institutions such as peace treaties and the trade system supplanted supernatural beings/powers as key referents of the social hierarchy symbology. In this process the Caddoan social hierarchy was collapsed, but through the repositioning of Europeans at the apex of an arrangement of means and powers by which well-being could be sustained, the principle of hierarchy was preserved as a deep-structural element of Caddoan culture. Instead of parallel hierarchies headed, respectively, by the Gran Xinesi and Ayo-Caddi-Aymay, the Caddoan repositioned their society within a single, secular hierarchy at the top of which now existed the Europeans and their political and economic institutions. Importantly, this structural transformation was probably not regarded by the Caddoan as a subjugation of their culture by Europeans. Rather, it was a way to incorporate Europeans (and the consequences of interacting with Europeans) into their own cultural categories, even as these categories underwent change.

In summary, Caddoan culture endured many changes as a result of contact with Europeans. Some of these changes were outwardly apparent while others represent more subtle transformations of deeper categories and relationships. But despite these many changes Caddoan culture was maintained as a distinctive and viable entity throughout the period considered in this study in the sense that deeply rooted values were preserved, including a social organization based on fundamental principles of hierarchy. The categorical distinctions and relationships constituting the traditional hierarchical system were revalued in the contact situation to incorporate the Europeans who had become a permanent part of the social scene. The revaluation enabled the Caddoan, for a time at least, to maintain cultural viability in the context of a world no longer controllable by traditional notions of order and balance.

NOTE

1. The accounts I have used refer primarily to the two largest Caddoan confederacies, the Hasinai and the Kadohadacho, but also frequently mentioned are the Natchitoches, Yatasis, and, to a lesser extent, the Cahinnio Caddo. For discussion of these and other Caddoan groups, see Swanton 1942.

REFERENCES

Bolton, H. E., 1912. The Spanish Occupation of Texas, 1519–1690. *Southwestern Historical Quarterly* 16:1–26.
_____, 1914. *Athanas de Mezieres and the Louisiana-Texas Frontier, 1768–1780.* 2 volumes (Cleveland: Arthur H. Clark Company).
_____, 1915. *Texas in the Middle Eighteenth Century.* Studies in Spanish Colonial History and Administration (Berkeley: University of California Press).
_____, 1939. *Wider Horizons of American History* (New York: D. Appelton-Century Company).
Boon, J. A., 1982. *Other Tribes, Other Scribes—Symbolic Anthropology in the Comparative Study of Cultures, Histories, Religions, and Texts* (Cambridge: Cambridge University Press).
Casis, L. M., 1899. Translation of Letter of Don Damian Manzanet to Don Carlos de Siguenza Relative to the Discovery of the Bay of Espiritu Santo. *Texas State Historical Association Quarterly* 2(4):253–312.
Falconer, T., trans., 1975. *On the Discovery of the Mississippi: With Translation from Original Manuscript of Memoirs Relating to the Discovery of the Mississippi by Robert Cavelier de la Salle and the Chevalier Henry de Tonti* (Austin: Shoal Creek Publisher).
Foik, P. J., 1933. Captain Don Domingo Ramon's Diary of His Expedition into Texas, 1716. *Texas Catholic Historical Society Preliminary Studies* 2(1).
French, B. F., 1869. *Historical Collections of Louisiana and Florida, Including Translations of Original Manuscripts Relating to Their Discovery and Settlement, with Numerous Historical and Bibliographic Notes . . . New*

Series (New York: J. Sabin & Sons). (Micropublished in *Western Americana: Frontier History of the Trans-Mississippi West, 1550–1900* [New Haven, Conn.: Research Publication, Inc., 1975].)

Geertz, C., 1973. *The Interpretation of Cultures* (New York: Basic Books).

Glover, W. B., 1935. A History of the Caddo Indians. *Louisiana Historical Quarterly* 18(4):872–946.

Griffith, W. J., 1954. *The Hasinai Indians of East Texas as Seen by Europeans, 1687–1772*. Philological and Documentary Studies 2(3) (New Orleans: Middle American Research Institute, Tulane University).

Hackett, C. W., 1931–46. *Pichardo's Treatise on the Limits of Louisiana and Texas*. 4 volumes (Austin: University of Texas Press).

Hatcher, M. A., trans., 1927. Descriptions of the Tejas or Assinai Indians, 1691–1722. *Southwestern Historical Quarterly* 30(3):206–218, 30(4):283–304, 31(1):50–62, 31(2):150–180.

Hoffman, F. L., ed. and trans., 1935. Fray Francisco Celiz: Diary of the Alarcon Expedition into Texas, 1718–1719. *Quivara Society Publications* 5.

Holder, P., 1967. The Fur Trade as Seen from the Indian Point of View. In *The Frontier Re-examined*, J. F. McDermott, ed. (Urbana: University of Illinois Press), pp. 129–139.

John, E. A. H., 1975. *Storms Brewed in Other Men's Worlds: The Confrontation of Indians, Spanish, and French in the Southwest, 1540–1795* (College Station: Texas A & M University Press).

Joutel, H., 1966. *The Last Voyage Performed by de la Salle* (Ann Arbor: University Microfilms). (Reprint of the edition first published in 1714.)

Kress, M. K., trans., 1931. Diary of a Visit of Inspection by the Texas Missions Made by Fray Gaspar José de Solis in the Year 1767–68. *Southwestern Historical Quarterly* 35(1):28–76.

Leach, E., ed., 1967. *The Structural Study of Myth and Totemism* (London: Tavistack).

Lewis, O., 1942. *The Effects of White Contact upon Blackfoot Culture* (Seattle and London: University of Washington Press).

Martin, C., 1978. *Keepers of the Game* (Berkeley: University of California Press).

Morfi, J., 1932. *Excerpts from the Memories for the History of the Province of Texas* (appendix, prologue, and notes by Frederick C. Chabot).

Newcomb, W. W., Jr., 1961. *The Indians of Texas, from Prehistoric to Modern Times* (Austin: University of Texas Press).

Sahlins, M., 1981. *Historical Metaphors and Mythical Realities, Structure in the Early History of the Sandwich Islands Kingdom* (Ann Arbor: University of Michigan Press).

Shea, J. D. G., 1852. *Discovery and Exploration of the Mississippi Valley, with the Original Narratives of Marquette, Allouez, Member, Hennepin, and Anastase Douay* (New York: Redfield).

Smith, R. A., trans., 1958–1959. Account of the Journey of Bernard de la Harpe: Discovery Made by Him of Several Nations Situated in the West. *Southwestern Historical Quarterly* 62(1):75–86, 62(2):246–259, 62(3):371–385.

Swanton, J. R., 1942. *Source Material on the History and Ethnology of the Caddo Indians.* Smithsonian Institution, Bureau of American Ethnology, Bulletin 132 (Washington, D.C.: Government Printing Office).

Turner, V., 1967. *The Forest of Symbols: Aspects of Ndembu Ritual* (Ithaca: Cornell University Press).

The Cherokee in Arkansas: An Invisible Archeological Resource

Hester A. Davis

In the very late eighteenth and early nineteenth centuries, small numbers of Cherokee Indians came west of the Mississippi River to get away from the pressures being placed on them from myriad sources in their homeland. Although there are a good many written records of various kinds about the thirty-some years in which they resided in different parts of Arkansas, we have yet to identify with assurance one Cherokee archeological site. The purpose of the research reported in this paper was to search the literature for possible answers to the following questions: Where should one look for sites where Cherokee lived? What should one look for at such sites? Will it be possible to tell these sites from non-Cherokee sites of the same time period?

The historical records tell us that by around 1790, some Cherokee, along with stragglers from other displaced eastern groups such as the Delaware and Shawnee, seem to have settled along the upper reaches of the St. Francis River in what is now southeastern Missouri and northeastern Arkansas (Figure 1). In 1794, some Cherokee killed a few whites at Muscle Shoals, Alabama, and as a consequence they and their families fled west of the Mississippi River into what was Spanish territory, joining others on the upper St. Francis River. The leader of this group was known as The Bowl (Clarke 1972). As far as we know, they continued to live there until the time of the New Madrid earthquake of 1811–12. They would have been very close to the center of that major quake and its aftershocks, and it is likely to have shaken them considerably in more ways than one. Some time in 1812 or 1813, The Bowl and his followers moved to the middle Arkansas River Valley to the south side of the river near Dardanelle. The reason for choosing this area must surely have been that there were Cherokee there

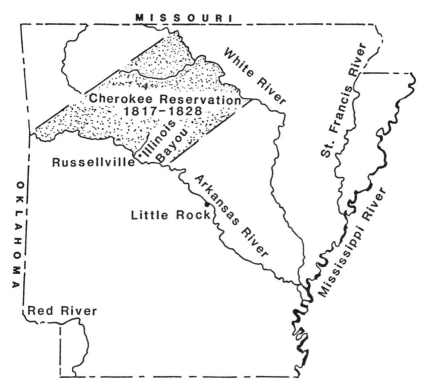

Figure 1
Cherokee Settlement Area in Arkansas, 1817–1828.

already. In 1808 or 1809, a Cherokee leader named Toluntuskee, having checked out the area earlier, brought several families (perhaps
numbering as many as three hundred people) from east Tennessee to
the area of Dardanelle Rock, a well-known landmark on the Arkansas
River. Toluntuskee is said to have settled on the north side of the river
in the vicinity of Galla Rock, which is downriver from Dardanelle and
Russellville about fifteen miles and where his brother, John Jolly, was
living in the 1820s (Vance 1970:13). Between 1809 and 1812, it is
variously recorded that between eleven hundred and fifteen hundred
Cherokee moved to this area of Arkansas (McLoughlin 1984:32, 75).
There was already a trading factory at Spadra, opened first in 1805
presumably for trade with both the Osage and the Cherokee.

The Arkansas River Valley in this area is fertile, mountains were available as in the Cherokee homeland for hunting and gathering, the tributaries from the north into the Arkansas River were full of fish, and the terrain in general would have looked quite a bit like home (although now it would be hardly recognizable). In 1813, Major Lovely was sent as Indian agent to the Cherokee, and his post was about a mile up Illinois Bayou on the north side of the Arkansas opposite Dardanelle Rock. Around 1821, when David Beardsley became agent, he moved the agency to the south side of the river close to Dardanelle Rock, where the "great Council Oaks" became a famous meeting place.

In 1817, a formal treaty, although contested, was negotiated by which land was exchanged in the Cherokee homeland for land in Arkansas and the Cherokee Reservation was created, encompassing almost all of the areas of the Arkansas Ozarks north of the river (see Figure 1). The boundary line on the east ran from the mouth of Point Remove Creek to a mountain just upstream from Batesville on the White River, and from approximately Fort Smith to the area of present-day Harrison. As a consequence, a large number of Cherokee from the east agreed to move to this area, the number given variously again as less than three thousand to more than five thousand (McLoughlin 1984). The majority of these settled in the vicinity of the earlier Cherokee and around the agency on Illinois Bayou, but there were some that are recorded as having been north of there on the Buffalo River and its tributaries and along the White River. One source (Lankford 1977:15) says, "The Cherokee were in two major locations—on Spring Creek off the Buffalo River and at Norfork." In addition, they also settled along other smaller tributaries going north from the river between Galla Rock on the east and the Mulberry River on the west (Turrentine 1962).

In 1818, at the invitation of Toluntuskee, the American Board of Commissioners for Foreign Missions arranged for two men to minister to the Arkansas Cherokee. Cephas Washburn and Alfred Finney arrived at Illinois Bayou in the summer of 1820, built two cabins, and before Christmas went back to Tennessee to pick up their families (Washburn 1869). By May 1821, they had returned and proceeded to create what became known as Dwight Mission, which over the next seven years grew to some thirty buildings, with seventy to eighty Cherokee children in attendance at the school (American Board of Commissioners for Foreign Missions [ABCFM] 1822, 1824, 1829).

In 1828, as a result of continual political maneuvering in the east and in accordance with the wishes of both Arkansas whites and the Cherokee, the Cherokee were moved again to the west almost two hundred miles to Indian Territory. The Cherokee Reservation in Arkansas was dissolved and the land again opened to white settlers. All the people involved with Dwight Mission moved at this time, and it has been presumed that all Cherokee moved as well. Those who moved from Arkansas were known to the Cherokee who came to Indian Territory in 1835 and 1836 as the "Old Settlers."

SOURCES

This, briefly, is the history of the Cherokee in Arkansas up to 1828 as one usually reads about it (Ferguson and Atkinson 1966). There are a few primary sources which help fill out this meager outline. Two of the principal ones are the Territorial Papers and the writings of Cephas Washburn and Alfred Finney in their reports and letters to the ABCFM. In addition, Thomas Nuttall, the noted botanist, visited the Cherokee in 1819 and describes them in a much-quoted paragraph (Nuttall 1905:174). There are a few, a very few, scattered letters by both Cherokee and whites that have been found from the period. There are reports from the Indian agents and from the factor at Spadra. All these sources leave a lot to be desired in any effort to gain a real picture of everyday life of the Cherokee in their Arkansas home, much less how we might be able to recognize them archeologically. The sources of greatest use are the Government Land Office (GLO) maps, although the reservation area itself was not surveyed until after 1829; the state and county historical societies' journals; and an excellent book-length history dissertation by Robert Markman entitled "The Arkansas Cherokee" (1972).

The realities of the situation soon become clear. It will take some minute searching of Washburn's and Finney's voluminous hand-written papers to try and pinpoint locations of possible Cherokee sites, and it will take direct archeological field work, preferably in the most populated area of occupation along Illinois Bayou and associated tributaries, to get a clue as to the lifeway of the Cherokee in the decades of 1810 and 1820. And even then, for the best and most obvious information, we are thirty years too late.

RESEARCH RESULTS TO DATE

In 1957, the Smithsonian Institution performed an archeological survey of the area to be inundated by the proposed Dardanelle Lake on the main stream of the Arkansas River and partway up some tributaries, including a large bay on Illinois Bayou. The River Basin Survey field work at that time did not include recording historic sites, as we do now. Dwight Mission is not mentioned in the report of the survey, and the original maps have only a pencil mark indicating where the mission cemetery is still located on a hill above the mission proper. A prehistoric site was thoroughly investigated directly across Illinois Bayou from where the mission must have been. The location of Lovely's agency and all of the area of the mission buildings is now under several feet of water, as are whatever other sites that might have been located up Illinois Bayou for five or six miles. No systematic surveys have ever been done specifically to try and locate Cherokee sites. However, G. R. Turrentine of Russellville, who singlehandedly wrote most of the *Arkansas Valley Historical Bulletin* for many years, has written in that publication of his efforts in the 1940s and 1950s to locate Dwight Mission and the saw and grist mill associated with it (Turrentine 1962). He found the location of both and it is likely that in his personal papers there may be a considerable amount of useful information about those sites, now destroyed by the lake and by Highway 64 across Mill Creek.

The Smithsonian archeologists did actually record one supposedly Cherokee site they heard about from a local informant in the process of getting information about prehistoric sites on his land. This site is in Johnson County on Big Piney Creek. In addition, an amateur historian from Searcy County believes he has found the location of one or two Cherokee sites along tributaries of the Buffalo River in that county (Johnston 1984). At the moment those are our extant records of known Cherokee archeological sites.

In a spurt of energy on a recent springlike Saturday, I went to Johnson County to see what the area looked like where the Smithsonian archeologists had indicated the Cherokee site was, but was not able to gain access to the property at that time. I was also looking for the location of an "Indian Plantation" so noted on the 1829 GLO map on Little Piney Creek. The GLO notes give no detail, only repeat those words which appear on the map. An arm of Dardanelle Lake creeps near this location, which is slightly rolling hills, sparsely populated, with small cleared pastures now—what A. L. Langham, the land surveyor, records as "Land a little uneven, soil 3rd rate, timber oak and hickory, undergrowth same arrow wood, etc." Sure enough, there is a historic site there in the right place, witnessed to by two depressions at the base of large trees, one with coursed stones and the other with field stones lying in and near the exposed roots of the trees and a nearby cedar tree with field stones around it and among its roots. There were no artifacts of any kind on the surface of the pasture, and further research in the county records must be done to provide some clue as to the possible date of this site. But the day did certainly encourage me, and I hope at least one graduate student, to think that it will be possible to locate sites of the period which have not been drowned by the lake.

What are the specific clues, then, as to possible location of sites of Cherokee settlement in the extant sources? As indicated, the GLO map of 1829 has two indications of possible sites along Big and Little Piney creeks and other possible sites along the Buffalo River on maps made in the 1830s. There is a lovely hand-drawn map of the area on both sides of the Arkansas River near Dardanelle Rock as it was in 1827, but the map was drawn from memory around 1880 during a land dispute (Russell Baker, personal communication); it has arrows to Cherokee settlements further up the tributaries than the map goes. The town of Dardanelle now covers the location of the agency shown on this map, but without doubt much remains in the soil there. Turrentine indicates that Finney's correspondence gives information on "Cherokee settlements on Point Remove Creek, Illinois Bayou, Big Piney, Little Piney, Spadra, Horse Head, and Mulberry" (Turrentine 1962:5). Indeed, by 1829 the *Missionary Herald* indicates that a second mission and school for the Cherokee had been established on Mulberry River, whence the preachers served seven Cherokee villages (ABCFM 1829). Other sources might bring us a little closer to possible sites. For example, Bowl and his followers were said to have been "between Shoal

and Petit Jean Creeks on the south side of the River" (Starr 1921);
another source says, "Chief Bowles' settlement was near the mouth of
Petit Jean Creek, about four miles from the Arkansas River, in what is
now Conway County, about ten miles northwest of present Perryville"
(Clarke 1972:13). Emmett Starr, the well-known historian of the Cherokee, says, "The capitol of the Cherokee Nation West from 1813 to
1824 was at Takatoka's village; from 1824 to 1828, it was at Piney on
Piney Creek" (Starr 1921:39–40). One early history of Pope County
reveals that "Chickalah's village was the site of the present town of
that name. John Jolly's village was at Galla Rock. Dutch's village was
on Dutch Creek, a tributary of Petit Jean River above Danville. Walter
Webber [a half-breed Cherokee who was said to be a chief and a well-
known trader] lived in what is called the 'London Bottoms' . . . Some
lived at Williamson's Ford on the Illinois Bayou, but others lived farther up the Illinois" (Vance 1970:13). One must take this source with a
grain of salt, since it goes on to say, "One of the largest Indian burial
grounds on the entire continent extends eastward from the foot of Nor-
ristown Mountain for miles along both sides of the Arkansas River"
(Vance 1970:17). There was a large prehistoric cemetery area which
was revealed by the 1927 floods south of the river and east of Dardanelle, but it was not Cherokee. Finally, a history student's master's
thesis in 1931 records: "John Jolly lived at the Galley . . . a large
Cherokee village north of the Arkansas River in what is now the southern part of Pope County. Little is known of the Galley, but it is mentioned by early travelers as being a large Indian village. It was about 15
miles below Dardanelle Rock, about the same location as Galley Rock,
an important boat landing" (Hurley 1931:12).

All of this does narrow the area to look at a little bit! Interestingly
enough, most references of the time talk of "settlements" and/or "villages." I am presuming that this means the kind of settlement pattern
found in the Cherokee homeland; that is, farmsteads scattered for several miles up and down a creek. The farmsteads are never described in
detail that I have been able to find to date, but Nuttall says,

> in their farms, which were well fenced and stocked with cattle, we
> perceive a happy approach toward civilization. Their numerous families,
> also, well fed and clothed, argue a propitious progress in their population.
> Their superior industry, either as hunters or farmers, proves the value of

property among them, and they are no longer strangers to avarice, and the distinctions created by wealth; some of them are possessed of property to the amount of many thousands of dollars, have houses handsomely and conveniently furnished, and their tables spread with our dainties and luxuries. (Nuttall 1905:174)

Washburn says, "The Cherokee were raising large stocks of horses, cattle and hogs, were building comfortable log-cabins, and beginning to cultivate the soil" (Washburn 1869:115). In 1837, Captain John Stuart described Cherokee houses: "The Cherokees form their buildings precisely like those of the frontier settlements of the United States. Their houses are, for the most part, cabins, covered with boards or shingles four feet long, and are confined by weight poles. Some of them are built of hewn logs; others are framed and weather boarded, and have good shingled roofs, plank floors, and in many cases, have good stone chimneys" (Stuart 1837:11). This description is presumably of the Cherokee in Indian Territory, although it is not altogether clear whether Stuart is describing the houses at the time he wrote or from some earlier observations. In any event, one surmises from this that the archeological sites will contain materials and features similar to any other non-Cherokee farmstead of the period.

However, there were activities carried on by the Cherokee which were not practiced by the whites and which would leave other kinds of possible evidence in the ground. Cephas Washburn is reported in the *Missionary Herald* (ABCFM 1822) as writing that on July 4, 1821 the Cherokee were planning to celebrate the "birthday of our national independence" and were "collected in a village near us for this purpose, but more especially for a war dance around the Osage scalp lately brought in with acclamations of joy." Lankford (1977:15) indicates there are records showing that the busk, or green corn ceremony, a ritual of thanksgiving (held in late summer when the late corn crop ripened), was celebrated by the Cherokee at the Norfork settlement on White River. Washburn also notes that a chief had asked him to select "twenty boys out of our school, to meet an equal number of boys from his village to play ball" (Washburn 1869:177). The archeologist must take this information to mean that near one of the farmsteads in a village will be an area where ceremonies and ball games would have taken place. How these latter kinds of sites may be manifested archeologically might be discerned from descriptions of them and the features which would have resulted from the activities in such sources as Mooney (1975) and Howard (1968).

Descriptions of material culture of the Cherokee in Arkansas are even more difficult to find in the contemporary literature. Washburn wished to stress to the Board of Commissioners how civilizing his school was for the Cherokee, and he seldom gives details of what must have been constant visits to Cherokee homes. In his reminiscences, only once does he describe a scene, this one at the time of his first meeting with Takahtokuh, a sixty-five-year-old chief:

> He set me a stool, and desired me to be seated; next he handed me a gourd of pure cool water and then said, "go and eat." On the *form,* which served in the place of a table, was an ample supply of wholesome food, cooked after the Indian custom, but palatable. I partook of it freely and with good relish, which seemed to afford the old chief great gratification, as he regarded it as an act of friendly communication . . . There was no plate on the *quasi* table, nor fork; a single knife, such as is usually carried by the Indians in their belts; and a spoon, manufactured by himself from buffalo horn, with which to help myself to hominy . . . were all the eating implements used. When my interpreter and myself had done sufficient justice to the viands before us, Takahtokuh filled his long pipe. (Washburn 1869:175–177)

Nothing in that description would distinguish a Cherokee cabin from that of the contemporary white people of the area or probably from those who immediately came into the area when the Cherokee left. One clue, however, is available which tells us that it is likely that in the Cherokee household ceramics may well still have been made and used. In recent excavations in contemporary nineteenth-century Cherokee sites in eastern Tennessee, local Cherokee pottery has been found in assemblages which would otherwise be indistinguishable from contemporary white occupations (Brett Riggs, personal communication).

SUMMARY

In conclusion, we know that Lake Dardanelle has inundated Dwight Mission and the remains of all its buildings; the saw and grist mill on Mill Creek has probably been destroyed by Highway 64 and Interstate

40; Lovely's original agency is also under Lake Dardanelle; a good many Cherokee farmsteads are also inundated, but a good many, without doubt, still remain in several areas within the original reservation. The major difficulty is going to be to recognize them as historic Cherokee. This will presumably be possible through the identification of those sites and features which were uniquely Cherokee; that is, the areas where ceremonies and ball games were held and farmstead sites which contain aboriginal-type ceramics as well as European goods. It may well be that the settlement system of the Cherokee will be a major identifying factor, with artifacts themselves a secondary factor.

In 1828, the Cherokee did not presumably simply abandon their houses and worldly goods; the latter they certainly took with them, and it may be that they dismantled some of the buildings as well. Some of this information may still be buried in the voluminous writings of Washburn and Finney. It seems likely that the white settlers would occupy the cleared land and any abandoned buildings, but the GLO maps and land records should be able to provide critical information as to land use and ownership immediately after 1829, which will be necessary in pinpointing individual sites as to the original occupation.

The areas south of the Arkansas River have not been affected by Dardanelle Lake as have those north, but reoccupation and particularly 150 years of farming will be a major problem there. Almost all cleared areas north of the river, including along the Buffalo and the White rivers, are now in pasture. It will take some real digging, both in the archival sources and in the ground, but I believe that it will be possible to identify more precisely some of the Cherokee sites and thereby make more visible Cherokee lifeways during their stay in Arkansas.

REFERENCES

American Board of Commissioners for Foreign Missions, 1822. *The Missionary Herald at Home and Abroad* (Boston: Report of the American Board of Commissioners for Foreign Missions from Documents Laid before the Board at the 13th Annual Meeting).

————, 1824. *The Missionary Herald at Home and Abroad* (Boston: Report of the American Board of Commissioners for Foreign Missions from Documents Laid before the Board at the 15th Annual Meeting).

————, 1829. *The Missionary Herald at Home and Abroad* (Boston: Report of the American Board of Commissioners for Foreign Missions from Documents Laid before the Board at the 20th Annual Meeting).

Clarke, Mary Whatley, 1972. *Chief Bowles and the Texas Cherokee* (Norman: University of Oklahoma Press).

Ferguson, John L., and J. H. Atkinson, 1966. *Historic Arkansas* (Little Rock: History Commission).

Howard, James, 1968. *The Southeastern Ceremonial Complex and Its Interpretation.* Missouri Archaeological Society, Memoir 6 (Columbia: Missouri Archaeological Society).

Hurley, William M., 1931. Socializing Forces in the History of Pope County, Arkansas. M.A. thesis, University of Arkansas.

Johnston, James J., 1984. Searcy County Indians in Tradition and History. *Mid-American Folklore* 12(1):24–31.

Lankford, George E., 1977. The Cherokee Sojourn in North Arkansas. *Independence County Chronicle* 18(2):2–19.

Markman, Robert, 1972. The Arkansas Cherokee:1817–1828. Ph.D. dissertation, University of Oklahoma.

McLoughlin, William G., 1984. *Cherokees and Missionaries, 1789–1839* (New Haven: Yale University Press).

Mooney, James, 1975. *Historical Sketch of the Cherokee* (Washington, D.C.: A Smithsonian Institution Press Book, Aldine Book Co.).

Nuttall, Thomas, 1905. A Journal of Travels into the Arkansas Territory, during the year 1819, with Occasional Observations on the Manners of the Aborigines. In *Early Western Travels, 1748–1846,* vol. 13, Reuben Gold Thwaites, ed. (Cleveland: Arthur H. Clark Co.).

Starr, Emmett, 1921. *History of the Cherokee Indians and Their Legends and Folklore* (Oklahoma City: Warden Co.).

Stuart, Captain John, 1837. *A Sketch of the Cherokee and Choctaw Indians* (typescript in Special Collections, University of Arkansas Library, Fayetteville; original publisher: Woodruff and Pew, Little Rock).

Turrentine, G. R., 1962. Dwight Mission. *Arkansas Valley Historical Papers* 25:1–11.

Vance, David L., 1970. *Early History of Pope County* (Mabelvale, Ark.: Foreman-Payne Publishers).

Washburn, Cephas, 1869. *Reminiscences of the Indians* (Richmond, Va.: Presbyterian Committee of Publications).

The Easter and Tug-of-War Lynchings and the Early Twentieth-Century Black Exodus from Southwest Missouri

Burton L. Purrington and Penny L. Harter

> . . . there is even now something of ill omen amongst us. I mean the increasing disregard for law which pervades the country—the growing disposition to substitute the wild and furious passions in lieu of the sober judgement of courts, and the worse than savage mobs for the executive ministers of justice.
>
> —Abraham Lincoln, *The Perpetuation of Our Political Institutions* (1837)

> Lynching is much more an expression of southern fear of Negro progress than of Negro crime. . . . [It] has always been the means for protection not of white women, but of profits.
>
> —Walter White, *Rope and Faggot* (1969)

> Lynching . . . like laws against intermarriage, masked uneasiness over the nature of white woman's desires. It aimed not only to engender fear of sexual assault but also to prevent voluntary unions. It upheld the comforting fiction that at least in relation to black men, white women were always objects and never agents of sexual desire.
>
> —Jacquelyn Dowd Hall, "The Mind that Burns in Each Body: Women, Rape, and Sexual Violence" (1984)

On April 15, 1903, in the southwestern Missouri mining town of Joplin, a black suspect in the killing of a white police officer was lynched by a mob of angry whites. That same evening the mob destroyed many of the homes and businesses in Joplin's black community and drove most blacks from the city. Joplin's civic leaders, many of whom tried to prevent the lynching, were frustrated and embarrassed by the incident and their chagrin was compounded by criticism from neighboring communities, notably their more cosmopolitan neighbor to the east, Springfield, whose newspapers condemned the rioting as "crazy, criminal acts" and "an outrage upon the innocent." Three years later, however, the chickens came home to roost in Springfield. On Easter Eve and in the early hours of Easter Sunday three young black men were hanged and their bodies burned and mutilated beyond recognition on Springfield's town square. This time Springfield gave its own black community little sympathy and made clear its feelings that the lynching victims and the city's blacks in general had it coming. As a result of these and other lynchings and acts of racial violence in southwest Missouri around the turn of the century many blacks left the region and blacks have not played a significant role there up to the present time.

Violent suppression of antisocial conduct, particularly that of minorities, has been part of American life since the earliest days of colonization. One of the most common forms of such social control has been lynching, the practice whereby mobs capture individuals suspected of a crime or take them from officers of the law and execute them without any process of law (Cutler 1969:1). According to statistics of the Tuskegee Institute, between 1882 and 1962 4,736 people were lynched in the United States and of that number 3,442 or 73 percent were blacks (Ploski and Williams 1983:347). However, blacks were not always the most common victims of lynching; before the 1870s more whites than blacks were lynched in this country. Lynching was viewed as a kind of frontier justice where court systems were not yet firmly established or where they were not regarded as a functioning form of justice (Cutler 1969:1–2). But the end of the Civil War brought the abolition of slavery and the passage of reconstruction reform measures which offered greater rights and opportunities to black Americans, and the black person in the South "ceased to be valuable as a property and was looked upon as a dangerous political factor in the community" (Cutler 1969:135). Control of blacks was considered essential to the preservation of the South's social, political, and economic status quo, and lynching became "an effective instrument to assure white dominance and the maintenance of a racial caste system" (McGovern 1982:5).

At the height of lynching in the United States (1882–1903), 93 black men and women were lynched on the average each year with the peak being reached in 1892 with 230 lynchings recorded (Cutler 1969:171). The alleged crimes for which blacks were lynched during this period include murder, 38 percent; rape, 34.3 percent; arson, 5 percent; theft, 4.9 percent; assault, 2.3 percent; desperadoism, 0.9 percent; unknown crimes, 4.3 percent; and minor offenses, 10.1 percent (Cutler 1969:175). "Minor offenses" include such departures from the norm as bringing suit against a white man, frightening school children, trying to act like a white man, strike-breaking, using offensive language, poisoning mules, and making boastful remarks (Raper 1969:36). In addition to real crimes against persons or property, then, lynchable offenses can be seen as "any mood or inclination among blacks deemed by whites to be anything less than complete subservience demanded by the master race" (Brown 1975:214)—in short, "uppitiness." Egerton notes that even in the relatively moderate racial climate of Tennessee after World War I "the most benevolent white citizens tended to be fearful of just two things: the social elevation of blacks, individually or collectively, and the prospect of a sexual attraction between black men and white women" (Egerton 1983:57). Blacks, then, were seen as serious threats on two fronts—political-economic and sexual—both of which have the common denominator of power relationships. Lynching provided white American society with a quick and effective solution to both problems which, despite its extralegal nature, was couched in moralistic terms. On the one hand, it served to keep blacks at the bottom level of the nation's social, political, and economic structure and to maintain a peonage system of tenant farmers and cheap (often prison) labor (Grant 1975). On the other, as early twentieth-century antilynching activist Jessie Daniel Ames, a southern white woman, emphasized, lynching also served as a mechanism for keeping not only blacks but white women in their place (Hall 1979).

Missouri, of course, is a border state, not Deep South, but lynching has been no stranger to it. In fact, the closeness of Missouri's cultural ties to the South is evident in the statistics on lynching. Of the 219 lynchings recorded in twenty-one "northern" states during the period 1889 to 1918 by the National Association for the Advancement of Colored People (NAACP) (1919:31), 81 or 37 percent occurred in Missouri. (The next closest northern states were Illinois with 24 lynchings and Kansas with 22.) Missouri also led such southern states as Delaware (1), Maryland (17), West Virginia (29), North Carolina (53), and Virginia (78) in lynchings during this thirty-year period and ranked twelfth in the nation (NAACP 1919:31–35).

Fifty-three or 65 percent of Missouri's lynching victims during this period were black (NAACP 1919:82), but there was a significant change in the racial identity of the victims over this period. From 1889 to 1897 in Missouri, 22 (57.9 percent) of those lynched were white and 16 (42.1 percent) were black. The pattern shifted dramatically between 1898 and 1902 when only 5 (22.7 percent) of those lynched were white and 17 (77.3 percent) were black. Between 1903 and 1918, 20 out of 21 people lynched in Missouri were black (NAACP 1919:80–82). It appears that lynching as a form of frontier justice ended around the turn of the century in Missouri but survived as an instrument of racial (and perhaps sexual) suppression for many years longer.

Murder and rape were the crimes of which the majority of Missouri's white and black lynching victims were accused (74 percent and 73 percent, respectively). However, black victims were accused of rape nearly twice as often as whites (25 percent to 14 percent) (NAACP 1919:80–82).

Lynchings during the 1889 to 1918 period were scattered over much of Missouri, but some geographical patterns are evident. Lynchings of individuals of both races occurred most commonly along the major river drainages of the state, the Mississippi and Missouri. Lynchings of whites were rather evenly distributed, whereas lynchings of blacks tended to concentrate in three areas: Missouri's "Little Dixie" along the Missouri River in the central part of the state; the Bootheel region in the extreme southeastern part of Missouri which had been part of the southern plantation economy; and the Ozark-prairie border of south-western Missouri where slavery had been practiced on a relatively small scale but prosouthern sentiments were strong during the Civil War. In 1880 and 1900 blacks in Missouri were most heavily concentrated in the Little Dixie and Bootheel regions, but except for Springfield their numbers were relatively few in the southwestern part of the state (Rafferty 1982:43).

Between 1889 and 1918, 12 men, of whom two-thirds or 8 were black, were lynched in southwest Missouri, but most state and local histories exclude references to these events and deal with the history of blacks in the region in a cursory manner, if at all. An exception is Shaner's *Story of Joplin* (1948), which describes both of Joplin's lynchings, a white man in 1885 and a black man in 1903. Even so, there is little local recollection of the latter event; of the half-dozen librarians, clerks, and older Joplin residents interviewed during the course of this study, none recalled that it had taken place in Joplin and some believed that it had occurred in a neighboring community. In a recent study of Missouri's black history, the Springfield lynching is referred to as "perhaps the most flagrant example [in Missouri] of this tragic violence against blacks" (Greene, Kremer, and Holland 1980:97), but there is little other discussion of the role of blacks in southwest Missouri in the book.

One of the first in-depth studies of blacks in southwest Missouri was a historical investigation of Springfield's Easter lynching in a 1970 master's thesis by Mary Clary. More recently, Katherine Lederer, an English professor at Southwest Missouri State University, has gone to the collections of memorabilia and oral histories of black and white families in Springfield to recover much of the city's "lost black history" (Lederer 1982). Finally, recent urban development in Springfield has included construction in areas presently or formerly occupied by blacks, and cultural resource management studies in these areas have led to the recovery of much valuable historical, archeological, and architectural data (Flanders, Harris, and Quick 1981; Harris 1981). However, the black history of the remainder of southwest Missouri, including Joplin, remains largely unexplored.

The following account of the Joplin lynching has been largely reconstructed from contemporary newspaper accounts and editorials supplemented by records in the U.S. Census and city directories. Efforts to locate important records of police and fire department logs, coroners' inquests, grand jury proceedings, and trials of alleged members of the lynch mob have been unsuccessful up to this point. Many of these records may no longer exist because Joplin's courthouse burned several years after the lynching; other records such as trial testimony simply may have been misplaced.

Newspaper accounts are, of course, a highly selective and often strongly biased source of information, particularly for events so emotion-charged and politically explosive as racial violence. Often news-

papers deliberately exaggerated the wrongdoings of blacks and under-
played those of whites in cases of racial conflict (Wood 1968:25–26).
For example, it is quite evident that the turn-of-the-century newspapers
in Joplin and Springfield, both Democratic and Republican, gave far
greater attention to crimes committed by blacks, especially petty
crimes such as the theft of lingerie or an oil lamp. Moreover, white
newspapers generally represented the white male social, economic,
and political establishment at the turn of the century and they had a
vested interest in maintaining the status quo not only in black-white
relations but in economic, class, and sexual relations as well. Recently
Howell (1983) demonstrated significant class-based differences between newspaper descriptions of the 1933 lynching of a rural, lower-
class white man in East Tennessee and perceptions of the event by
relatives and acquaintances of the victim.

However, if we look at newspaper accounts as *interpretations* of
events rather than God's truth, we are on much firmer ground. When
we are attempting to understand the cultural context of a particular
period, the accuracy of the reporting of specific events, though important, often becomes secondary to how those events were perceived or
how their reporting was manipulated by one group or another to serve
various ends. In the case of the Joplin lynching, we are fortunate to
have accounts and opinions from several newspapers of vastly different
political and ideological persuasions. The perspectives derived from
these newspapers give us important insights into the nature of the
culture of Joplin and southwest Missouri at the turn of the century and
they help us better understand why blacks play such a limited role in
the region today.

The major sources for the following reconstruction of the Joplin
lynching were the *Joplin Daily Globe* (hereafter referred to as *Globe*),
a Democratic paper, and the *Joplin Daily News-Herald* (hereafter referred to as *News-Herald*), a Republican paper. Several other local and
regional newspapers provided information too.

During the 1890s and early 1900s Joplin, a mining town on the
prairie near the Kansas border, was a regional hub of growth and development. After a two-year depression, Joplin's economy was booming again by 1895 when zinc and lead prices rose dramatically. Between 1890 and 1900 Joplin's population increased from 10,000 to
26,000. Joplin's black population during this period was not large;

only 773 or 3 percent of the city's residents recorded in the 1900 census were black. However, despite their relatively small numbers, many blacks were actively participating in Joplin's booming economy. Most were laborers and domestics, but some owned their own businesses such as barbershops and at least one served on the city police force.

Notwithstanding their economic gains, however, the city's blacks were still socially and politically restricted. They were segregated in two neighborhoods. One, called Kansas City Bottom, was on the north side of town and included mostly low-income blacks and whites as well as a sizable number of unemployed people, professional criminals, and transients. The north side of town, black and white, was associated with violence, crime, and bawdy houses. Joplin's black middle class lived apart from Kansas City Bottom on the east side of town. The black vote was largely controlled by the Democrats.

Considering the fact that Joplin was a rough and tumble mining town, the events leading up to the killing of the police officer and the subsequent lynching probably were fairly routine. On Tuesday evening, April 14, 1903, Officer Theodore Leslie of the Joplin city police (Figure 1) reported to the night officer, Captain Loughlin, that he had received a report that two black men with guns were at the Kansas City Southern railroad yard in the Kansas City Bottom. Leslie suspected that they may have been involved in a theft of guns and ammunition from the Bullock & Pierce Hardware Store or the robbery of a physician, both of which had taken place in Joplin the night before. Shortly before Leslie's arrival at the police station, Captain Loughlin had been visited by Sam Bullock, the hardware store owner, and a black man who had informed Bullock that the men who had robbed his store were at the Kansas City Southern yards. Loughlin sent Officer Ben May along with Bullock and the black informer to the railroad yard, and when Leslie arrived and delivered his report shortly thereafter, Loughlin sent him to assist May and the others.

However, Leslie did not find his fellow officer immediately and about 7:30 P.M. he was seen by several eyewitnesses searching around the yards. When he reached a string of boxcars off to the side on a holding track, he spotted a black man on the other side of a car. Leslie stopped him, but as he began to search him a shot was fired, apparently from inside one of the boxcars. Leslie returned the fire, and the black man he had been searching fled only to be stopped and arrested. Iron-

OFFICER THEODORE LESLIE KILLED

Brave Officer Shot and Instatnly Killed
By a Tramp Negro---Two Bullets
Pierce His Body and the Negro
Makes His Escape.

HOUNDS ON TRAIL OF THE ASSASSIN

Hundreds of Men With Guns Followed, But at a Late Hour the
Hounds Had Not Been Suc-
cessful.

OFFICER THEODORE LESLIE.

Figure 1
Headlines from the *Joplin Daily Globe*, April 15, 1903.

ically, he was taken to jail by a black former police officer, Cy Landis.

At least eight shots were exchanged between Leslie and his unknown assailant before Leslie was struck in the chest and the right eye
and killed instantly. Immediately, a black man jumped out of the boxcar and ran north along the tracks. Ike Clark, a white seventeen-year-
old carpenter, and several others gave chase. Clark came within fifteen
feet of the fleeing suspect, and they exchanged several shots. The other
pursuers later reported that all of the shots were wild, but Clark claimed
to have hit the suspect, and other witnesses reported seeing him slow
down and start to limp after he had outdistanced his pursuers.

The news of Leslie's killing spread rapidly through the city and the
surrounding area and a posse was organized to track down the suspect.
The *Globe* reported (April 15, 1903, p. 1) that "a crowd of fully 500
people had assembled at the jail eager to follow the hounds." The
search that evening was unsuccessful in part because Joplin's marshal
Burl Robison was "a rather large man" and the bloodhounds had to be
held back continually in order to maintain his pace. Disgusted with the

slowness of the pace and the fact that they had not been provided with rigs to speed them along, Webb City's marshal Marquiss, who had provided the hounds, took his dogs and men home about 11:00 P.M.

The following morning Officer Leslie's death was reported in front-page headlines. The *Globe* and Democratic mayor-elect T. W. Cunningham each offered $100 rewards for the capture and conviction of the killer. Later that day a suspect was captured. About 4:00 P.M. Lee Fullerton, an employee of the Bauer Brothers' Butcher Shop, and M. R. Bullock, a laborer, delivered a wounded black man with a serious gunshot wound to the leg whom they had captured at knife point to the Joplin city jail.

Officer Frank Belford began questioning the suspect as soon as he was secured in a cell. It was learned that he was Thomas Gilyard, age twenty-three, who had arrived in Joplin two nights earlier from Mississippi. Gilyard explained that he had been in the boxcar from which the shots that killed Leslie had come but that he had not done the shooting. He said there were three other men in the car, but since he had only been in Joplin for a day at that time he knew nothing about them. At this point the questioning was interrupted by a growing disturbance outside the cell.

While Gilyard was being questioned, news spread rapidly through the city and surrounding towns that Leslie's killer had been caught. Search parties had been scattered throughout the countryside, and excitement already was running high when word of the capture came out. Small groups of men, women, and children flocked to the jail, and within thirty minutes the surrounding streets were jammed with an estimated two thousand people. Hearing shouts of "Get a rope!" "Hang the nigger!" from the crowd, the officers placed Gilyard in a separate cell away from the other prisoners. Should the mob break into the jail, the officers did not want the wrong prisoner taken.

In a belated attempt to limit the growth and rowdiness of the crowd, Mayor Trigg ordered all of Joplin's saloons to close down for two hours, and the city attorney, Perl Decker, stepped outside the jail to address the mob. Decker asked the people in the crowd to be patient and allow the law to take its own course. Gilyard's guilt or innocence was not yet a certain fact, he said. Time was all that he was asking from the crowd, and he assured the people that Leslie's murderer would be brought to justice. Many of the people in the crowd heeded Decker's plea, and groups of them began to disperse. The situation appeared to be under control.

Suddenly, a new set of leaders emerged and demanded Gilyard's neck. The mob quickly regrouped around them. Disregarding pleas for patience from city officials, men began bringing lumber poles to be used as battering rams against the jailhouse doors. After failing to break down the iron door to the police courtroom, the mob redirected its energies to a side wall, which gave way. Rushing into the jail, the mob leaders pushed the police officers out of the way, broke into Gilyard's cell, and dragged him outside. Newspaper reports of Gilyard's behavior when he was seized were contradictory. The *Globe* (April 16, 1903, p.1) reported that Gilyard "fought like a demon," while the *News-Herald* (April 16, 1903, p. 1) claimed that he cowered in a corner and "cried like a baby."

Once outside with the prisoner, the mob surged up Second Street. All along the way Gilyard protested his innocence even though he was "beaten and cuffed and trampled and choked until he could no longer stand without assistance" (*Globe,* April 16, 1903, p. 2). At the intersection of Second and Wall streets, about two blocks from the jail, the crowd halted and men and boys began climbing trees and roofs to get a good view.

However, the man who was carrying the rope had been left far behind in the swell of the crowd, and while he was catching up Attorney Decker and several others once again attempted to dissuade the mob. Pleading with the crowd to allow Gilyard to be taken back to his cell to await a fair trial, Decker rode his horse into the crowd with Ike Clark behind him. Clark stated that Gilyard was not the man with whom he had exchanged gunfire at the railroad yard. Mayor-elect Cunningham and several others also tried to persuade the crowd to take Gilyard back to his cell so that justice could be done, but the mob leaders were not moved. After questioning Gilyard themselves in what amounted to a mock trial, they tied the rope around his neck and a man climbed a telephone pole with the rope, passed it over a cross-arm, and dropped it back into the crowd.

Then one of the most unusual and courageous efforts in the "red record" of lynching occurred. Those trying to prevent the lynching had not yet given up. Apparently without physical support from the police, with the possible exception of Ben May, a dozen or more men risked their lives and reputations in an attempt to save Gilyard. One of them cut the rope, but it was spliced and, when someone attempted to cut it again, he was driven back with a gun. Then, with shouts of "nigger lovers" in their ears, they grabbed the rope just above Gilyard's neck and tried to keep the mob from hauling him off the ground. Newspapers described the next few moments as a "tug-of-war," but the numbers in the mob were too great and Gilyard was pulled into the air and died of strangulation.

In contrast with a common theme in lynchings, Gilyard's body was not mutilated. The mob broke up shortly after the hanging, but about two hours later the saloons opened, thirsty patrons flocked to them, and small groups of men began to gather on street corners. The police and Mayor-elect Cunningham urged them to go home, but they were unsuccessful (*Globe*, April 16, 1903, p. 1). Soon a new mob had formed which converged on the jail and secured the release of the one man arrested after the lynching (for firing a gun) when they threatened to blow up the jail. Then they went to the Joplin Undertaking Company to demand Gilyard's body, but, anticipating trouble, Deputy Coroner Potter had already had the body removed. The mob then turned its vengeance on the black community. First they went to black-owned businesses and businesses that employed large numbers of blacks and ordered them out of town. Then they moved northward to the low-income and transient black neighborhood in the Kansas City Bottom where they attacked blacks with rocks and fists and set many houses on fire. The Joplin Fire Department attempted to control the flames, but streets were blocked, rocks were thrown at them, and hoses were cut by the mob and the firemen were forced to retreat. Soon the mob moved to the east side of town where it attacked the middle-class black neighborhood. Many life-long and respected black residents of Joplin lost their homes and virtually all of their possessions that night, but, miraculously, no one was killed.

To escape the wrath of the mob, about half of Joplin's black residents fled to neighboring communities and homes in the country (*Globe*, April 17, 1903, p. 2). Many did not return, and Joplin's black community never regained the relative economic success it had enjoyed prior to the lynching and riots.

Local reactions to the lynching and the rioting were mixed. The

Globe and the *News-Herald* both condemned the lawless violence and the usurpation of justice, but the *News-Herald* was considerably more muted in its criticism and expressions of concern for Joplin's dispossessed blacks. Moreover, the *News-Herald* took advantage of the opportunity to promote its party's law-and-order stance by blaming the violence on lax law enforcement by the incumbent Democrats and, in an editorial entitled "A Word for the Negro," lectured the city's blacks on their social responsibilities, saying:

> The negroes can learn a lesson from this. If they expect to be respected and aided in life, here or elsewhere, by the better class of whites upon whom they depend for employment, they must be industrious, truthful and courteous and they must omit much of the impudence often practiced. If they do this, they have the same opportunities to succeed in life as whites of equal ability, and they will be protected and respected by the better class of the white people.
> Will the negro see the point?

It should be noted that the *News-Herald*'s position was mild compared to that of the *Peirce City Empire* (the spelling of "Peirce" is correct). A year and a half before the Joplin lynching, three black men who had been accused of raping and murdering a young white woman were lynched, and all blacks were driven from the town never to return. In a series of editorials spanning several days, the *Empire* attacked blacks, Joplin's past tolerance of them, and critics of Peirce City's racist attitudes. Several of these editorials, including the most virulent (Figure 2), were reprinted in the *News-Herald*.

Three years later, almost to the day, southwest Missouri was seized again by brutal racial violence, this time in Springfield. It is instructive to compare the Joplin and Springfield lynchings.

Recent ethnohistoric and archeological investigations indicate that Springfield's turn-of-the-century black community was relatively affluent, somewhat independent economically, and politically influential. In Springfield, blacks had been physicians, attorneys, policemen, and businessmen and had served on the city council and school board (Lederer 1982). Springfield's largest grocery store, Hardrick's Grocery, was black-owned and -operated. A local bicycle shop operator, Walter ("Duck") Majors, won more than a dozen U.S. patents for his inventions and handcrafted one of the first automobiles seen in southwest Missouri. Of the 1,053 black adults listed in the 1906 Springfield

"A Good Nigger in Joplin"

(Peirce City Empire.)

The black brute who shot to death Officer Leslie in Joplin Tuesday night was hanged by a crowd of righteous citizens in that town Wednesday and another name has been added to the list of good negroes. This is another case where the creators of the law have shown the good sense necessary to prove that the people are supreme and the lives of honest citizens must be protected from the brutes of creation. The idea that a beast is any less a beast because it has evoluted until it bears a small resemblance to a human being, preposterous as it is, appears to have obtained such a hold upon a portion of society that nothing short of drastic measures will insure the protection to which people who compose that portion of society that has to follow an occupation of one kind or another is entitled.

It is a well established fact that officers of the law and men and women who labor for a living and their daughters are considered the legitimate prey of these descendants of the orangoutang. A score and a half years spent in an endeavor to make the negro believe he is no better that a laboring white man or his wife or daughter has filled thousands of graves with promising female loveliness and wrecked countless numbers of happy homes.

A year and a half ago when the murderers of an innocent young lady expiated their crime in this city and the rest of their race undertook to get revenge and were driven out as a result, Joplin extended to them a cordial welcome and, by acts, if not by words said "come here and rob and murder to your hearts' content." Joplin, having "sown to the wind," has now commenced to "reap the whirlwind."

Figure 2

Editorial in the *Peirce City Empire* printed two days after the lynching of Thomas Gilyard. In August 1901, three black men had been lynched in Peirce City for the alleged rape and murder of a young white woman. Subsequently, all blacks were driven from the town and ordered never to return. Many of the black refugees moved to Joplin. (Reprinted in the *Joplin Daily News-Herald,* April 19, 1903.)

city directory, 868 or 82.4 percent listed an occupation. Roughly 5 percent of this group can be classified as professionals (school principals and teachers, one attorney), business proprietors, semiprofessionals (pastors, musicians, firemen, etc.), or business employees (clerks, bookkeepers); 15 percent were skilled workers; and 80 percent were employed in service occupations or as unskilled laborers. Relative affluence at some black households is suggested by the presence of porcelain and decorated ceramics in archeological deposits at a black neighborhood in roughly equal proportions to nearby upper- and middle-class white neighborhoods and in much greater frequency than in nearby working-class white neighborhoods (Harris 1981:108–112).

Springfield's blacks were also numerically significant at this time. In 1890, one-third of the city's registered voters were black (Lederer 1982:11), and the 1900 census shows that about three thousand of the city's thirty thousand citizens were black. As a result of their political clout, blacks had served on the city council and school board and they were a powerful voting bloc courted by both parties but, unlike Joplin's blacks, generally Republican in allegiance.

Despite the accomplishments of many of Springfield's blacks and their political influence, they were still segregated and subjugated by Jim Crow laws and most worked for whites in some menial capacity (Clary 1970:2). Local public opinion was both reflected and influenced by the city's two newspapers, of which the *Republican* was benignly paternalistic while the *Leader,* the Democratic newspaper, was blatantly racist. Another problem area was Springfield's active business in pleasure—saloons, billiard parlors, and "sporting houses" provided an environment in which race relations were especially tense. Of particular cause for alarm in much of the white community was the public consorting of black men with white women. In the evenings young black men would buy whiskey at the back doors of local saloons, pick up their white "dates," and make a show of driving around town with them in buggies (Clary 1970:2–3).

The growing racial tension in the city was brought to a head by a combination of circumstances. One precipitating factor was a white police officer, Jesse Brake, who had a personal grudge against blacks because his wife had fallen in love with a black man and become pregnant by him. In 1904, Brake began distributing racist pamphlets which condemned the "beastly lust" of black men and argued that the justice of the mob was preferable to that of the courts in dealing with accused black rapists. The *Leader* (October 31, 1904, p. 5) legitimized Brake's "treatise" by publishing it. It should be noted that when John Mc-Cracken, the black man by whom Brake's wife had become pregnant, was jailed on suspicion of rape, two attempts were made by masked men to lynch him, but he was "spirited away" by the sheriff (Clary 1970:6). Ultimately, McCracken and Brake's ex-wife married.

A second set of critical circumstances was the murders of two white men in Springfield, allegedly by blacks, in December 1905 and January 1906. These led the *Leader* to amplify the savagery of its attacks on the "Negro race" and to warn blacks to behave or suffer the consequences (*Leader*, January 16, 1906, p. 4; January 26, 1906, p. 4). Well aware of the increasingly dangerous racial climate and the vulnerability of their position, Springfield's black leaders publicly deplored the violence; exhorted other blacks to work hard, behave, and be good Christians; and urged whites to be tolerant (*Republican*, February 13, 1906, pp. 2–3). However, tension continued to mount, heightened by a series of minor racial incidents, "all of which were over-played by the newspapers" (Clary 1970:7).

Ironically, the final contribution to the mounting racial tensions preceding the lynching was not criminal but political. In a city election first week of April 1906, the incumbent chief of police, J. R. McNutt, a Democrat, lost to Republican Acy Loveless by 275 votes. Since the majority of Springfield's 519 registered black voters voted Republican, it was generally assumed that they had swung the vote to Loveless, a sentiment that was reflected in the newspapers. The newspapers further speculated that there would be a clean sweep in the city police department and, possibly, the appointment of some black police officers (Clary 1970:7–8). It is reasonable to speculate that these events brought the racial hostility of Springfield's all-white police force to the boiling point.

The Springfield lynching has been described in detail by Clary (1970) and Lederer (1981a, 1981b), and the events will only be summarized here. On the evening of April 13, Good Friday, 1906, two young black men, Horace Duncan and Fred Coker, both of whom had grown up in Springfield and who had no criminal records, were arrested for the rape of a farmwife who reportedly had just moved to Springfield looking for work. The woman's companion, Charles

Cooper, a twenty-two-year-old hotel clerk, had reported to two police officers (one of whom was later indicted along with a brother of the second officer for participating in the lynching) that he had been escorting Mina Edwards to a new job when they were attacked by two masked black men who knocked him out and dragged her into a field and raped her. The next morning Coker and Duncan were arrested. Despite the masks of the alleged attackers and the dark night, Cooper claimed to have recognized Duncan and, since Coker worked with Duncan, he was arrested too. However, their boss at the Pickwick Livery and Transfer Company, Tom Morrow, a white man, came forward immediately to state that both men had been at work when the alleged attack took place. They were released, but, incredibly, they were arrested again that afternoon when Cooper filed a complaint that Duncan had stolen his watch during the alleged attack.

Rumors of a lynch mob had been circulating since early that morning, but Sheriff John Horner at the county jail where Duncan and Coker were locked up took no precautionary measures other than to call outlying communities to see if any out-of-town men were coming in and the city jail to see if they knew of any trouble. There were no reports of outsiders being on their way, and the recently defeated city police chief McNutt assured Horner that all was calm—even after the mob had passed the city jail on its way to take the prisoners.

About 9:00 P.M., the mob, which had been drinking heavily and had attacked white-owned stores and a white-occupied streetcar on the way, reached the jail. Although the deputies wanted to fire on the mob when it attacked the jail, Sheriff Horner ordered them not to because "innocent people might get hurt" (this despite the fact that his own home adjacent to the jail was being torn apart and his family terrorized by the mob). One police officer passing by attempted to dissuade the mob, and a visiting St. Louis attorney threw the gas switch for the lights in the jail hoping to frighten the mob away, but in the absence of any resistance from the sheriff the mob broke into Coker and Duncan's cell, beat them with sledge hammers (possibly killing Coker), and dragged them to the town square where they were hanged from a tower (with the goddess of liberty at the top) and their bodies burned and mutilated beyond recognition. Afterward, in the early morning hours of Easter Sunday, the mob returned to the jail and dragged Will Allen, one of the two blacks accused in the most recent murder of a white man in Springfield, to the square where he too was hanged and his body burned and mutilated. Throughout this time, local policemen were reported to have been standing on the edge of the mob conversing and laughing but making no attempt to interfere with the hangings or the mutilations.

Subsequently, it was revealed that Coker and Duncan's accusers, Mina Edwards and Charles Cooper, had spent the evening of the alleged rape at a local "sporting house," and that Mrs. Edwards had in fact left her husband and moved to Springfield a month earlier where she reportedly had been living a less-than-chaste life. Based on Tom Morrow's statement that Duncan and Coker had been working for him at the time of the alleged rape and Mrs. Edwards' confused and conflicting statements, even the police were forced to admit that the two lynching victims were "probably innocent" and a grand jury found likewise (Lederer 1981b:24).

The public outrage and shock that some of Springfield had expressed after the Joplin lynching were considerably more muted in the wake of what some were calling (in jubilation, not irony) Springfield's "Easter Offering." Fortunately, Springfield's black community was spared the destruction that had followed the Joplin lynching, but this seems to have been due to rumors that a friendly white quarry operator had helped blacks lay dynamite along the streets into their neighborhoods, to the formation of black "vigilance committees," and to a St. Louis hardware store owner, Arch McGregor, who organized a force of special deputies which dispersed a mob of three hundred forming on the town square to burn out the blacks and patrolled the black neighborhoods until the state militia arrived on Monday (Lederer 1981a:35).

The Springfield newspapers found the racial violence regrettable, but made it clear that they thought that the blacks had brought it on themselves. The more moderate *Republican* essentially ended its past paternalistic support of the city's blacks when it said, "The latent but true cause of the riot was race hatred. Constant complaints have been made for years that the Negroes of the city are insolent. Such tales . . . gradually formed a basis of hatred that finally bore fruit. . . . Let the Negroes ask themselves who is responsible for the rise of the opinion that 'the insolent element would have to be terrorized' " (*Republican*, April 17, 1906, p. 2, quoted in Lederer 1981a:36).

Although Springfieldians claimed that the mob was made up of out-of-towners and local hoodlums and riffraff, it is clear that the city's involvement ran much deeper. Among those arrested or indicted for participation in the lynching were several active and former police officers, including Jesse Brake, and the sons of two prominent Springfield businessmen. Moreover, the indictments and testimony showed that while the "riffraff" happily joined in the lynching, the mob was led by workmen, farmers, and small storekeepers (Lederer 1981a:36). Significantly, local judges, attorneys, city officials, and wealthy businessmen immediately stepped forward to post bond and supply counsel for those accused of involvement in the lynching. Community opinion ran strongly in favor of the accused, and acquittal was a foregone conclusion when the first of them was brought to trial. It is perhaps remarkable that, rather than finding for acquittal, the jury was hopelessly hung by two members who held out for a guilty verdict. The judge declared a mistrial, and eventually the prosecution, seeing no hope for a conviction, dropped charges against all of the accused.

In many ways, the Joplin and Springfield lynchings followed a nationwide, particularly southern pattern. There were the immediate assumptions that a black accused of a crime against a white person was guilty, rapidly growing rumors of a lynching, inadequate efforts to safeguard the prisoner, small gatherings of local men which quickly coalesced into a mob, the siege of the county jail, the unwillingness of the police to fire into the crowd or over their heads, the torture of the doomed prisoners (although not nearly as calculated, cruel, or prolonged as many incidents in the Deep South), and the subsequent attacks or attempted attacks on the black community. Moreover, in both cities the newspaper whose political party controlled the black vote exercised a paternalistic tolerance of blacks, whereas the papers whose party was out of favor with blacks were benignly to openly racist.

However, the Joplin lynching departs in several respects from the norm where Springfield holds true. Ironically, since Joplin had a reputation for being a rough and tumble, often violent mining town (a stereotype that has lasted to this day), it was here that the more active resistance to the mob took place, including the final heroic but futile attempt to save Thomas Gilyard's life. A dozen or more men risked their lives (and some their political careers) attempting to preserve law and order. Moreover, the Joplin mob did not mutilate Gilyard's body or collect ghastly trophies from his remains (although they did try to reclaim it after giving it up).

Furthermore, in Joplin it appears that the police offered at least token resistance to the mob (despite the fact that one of their own had been killed), and there is no evidence that any of them were actively involved in the mob as was the probable case in Springfield. In addition, although the general response to the lynching was mixed in Joplin, with many people feeling that Gilyard was guilty and got what he deserved, there was considerable public remorse over the rioting and destruction of property in the black sections of town. However, there is little evidence that such concern was translated into civic attempts to stop the flight of blacks from the city or bring back those who had fled, although two weeks after the lynching construction began on a new A.M.E. Church "from the funds donated to the colored people of Joplin by Thomas Connor," a local white businessman (*Globe,* April 26, 1903, p. 8).

Finally, in a very unusual departure from the norm, one of the leaders of the Joplin lynch mob was convicted. Sam Mitchell, a local laborer, was found guilty of second-degree murder for throwing the rope from which Gilyard was hanged over the telephone pole and he was sentenced to ten years in prison. Subsequently, however, Mitchell's conviction was overturned on the basis of alleged prejudicial statements made by one of the jurors prior to the trial, a second defendant was acquitted, and the third man arrested in connection with the lynching does not appear to have been brought to trial (*Globe,* June 2–5, 7, 17–18, 21, 23, 1903).

In the final account, the Joplin lynching seems to have been a relatively spontaneous event perhaps precipitated in part by bad feelings following very recent Republican election losses and Republican accusations of voter fraud by blacks (Figure 3), an increasing concern with local crime and the role of transients like Gilyard in it, and reports of lynchings and predicted lynchings elsewhere (Figure 4). On the other hand, Springfield's Easter lynching was, at the very least, something that many whites had been anticipating (even looking forward to) for a long time. The racial climate in Springfield seems to have been different both in degree and in kind from that in Joplin. Qualitatively, blacks in Springfield constituted a much larger minority than in Joplin (10 percent to 3 percent), and criminal accusations of blacks, particularly for serious crimes, were much more common in Springfield. There were important qualitative differences, too, in that Springfield's blacks were much more successful and competitive in the economic sphere,

DARKTOWN DEMOCRACY DOIN'S

Beneath the glare of scores of incandescent lamps, it is reported, Chief of Police Thomas J. Cofer, assisted by that undisputed leader of colored Democracy, Moses Brown, who at present is out of the calaboose on a furlough, banqueted the good negro Democrats of the city last night. If the rumors, which come from authentic sources, are correct, the elaborate affair took place in the rooms over Homer's saloon at the corner of Second and Main streets.

Unfortunately, a menu of the spread could not be obtained as Mr. Cofer had nothing to say on the matter. Nor could any of the speeches rendered be secured. But that there was a large gathering there is no doubt. The spacious hall, it is said, was crowded to its greatest seating capacity. Joplin's dark town society and political enthusiasts were there. Around the festal board, so the report has it, were gathered some of the foremost negro Democrats of the town. But there were also a few Republicans there and that is how the news of the meeting leaked out. In all, the event was one of the grandest of its kind in the political history of the city and although the little gathering was intended to be carried through on the "Q. T.," as long as the cat is out of the bag, Mr. Cofer's admirers will undoubtedly be glad to hear of the Democratic nominee's strenuous efforts.

As the News-Herald informant said, doesn't the Bible teach us to feed the raven and the black sheep?

$10 REWARD

Ten dollars reward will be paid to any person for any information leading to the arrest and conviction of anyone who has fraudulently registered or induced or attempted to induce anyone to so fraudulently register.

Or for any information leading to the arrest and conviction of any illegal voter, voting or attempting to vote at this coming election, or for anyone offering or accepting bribes, or for anyone using threats or intimidation to keep any legal voter from the polls.

Dated this 2d day of April.

REPUBLICAN CENTRAL COMMITTEE,
O. P. M. Wiley, Chairman.

Figure 3
In an effort to embarrass the Democrats five days before the upcoming city elections, the *News-Herald* published an exposé of Democratic wooing of local black voters. There is little doubt as to the reason for the juxtaposition of the exposé and the announcement of a reward for information leading to convictions for voter fraud. Two blacks had been arrested recently for attempting to buy votes and illegally register black voters, and the *News-Herald* was running the announcement frequently. (*News-Herald*, April 2, 1903.)

WILL BE BURNED AT THE STAKE

A Barbecue in Prospect for a Brutal Ravisher and Murderer in a Southern Town.

Bloodhounds Are on the Track of a Fiend Who Assaulted and Killed Mrs. Frank Matthews and Her 10-Year-Old Daughter.

SHREVEPORT, LA., April 11.— Mrs. Frank Matthews, wife of a civil engineer, and her 10-year-old daughter, Allene, were assaulted by an unknown person at their home near Anniston today.

Mrs. Matthews' head was crushed and she died later.

The girl is dying, her skull having been fractured and her chest crushed in.

Mrs. Matthews had considerable jew-elry on her person which was untouch-ed.

A posse with blood hounds is in pur-suit of the assailant who will doubtless be burned at the stake if captured.

No More Gambling at Denver

DENVER, April 11.—The police board of the city has issued orders that no more public gambling will be per-mitted here, and as a consequence the gambling houses of the city have closed.

Figure 4
Lurid descriptions of brutal crimes were common in turn-of-the-century newspapers. Often a prediction was made that the criminal would be lynched—particularly if the alleged criminal was black. This article appeared two days before Officer Theodore Leslie was killed. (*News-Herald*, April 12, 1903.)

they wielded much greater political influence, and they appear to have been much more open in their relations with white women. Therefore, Springfield's blacks constituted real and direct threats to the city's political and economic status quo as well as to the white man's sense of paternalism toward his women and the white male self-image. The fears that these threats generated were translated into accusations of insolence, uncontrollable lust, and criminality, and by 1906 the climate in Springfield was ripe for racial violence. Race relations in Springfield had followed a common post-reconstruction pattern and come to a predictable conclusion: "Periodically there seems to develop a situation in which a number of negroes begin to rebel against the caste restrictions. This is not an open revolt but a gradual pressure in which, little by little, they move out of the strict pattern of approved behavior. [Whites] say the negroes are getting "uppity," that they are getting out of their place, and that something should be done about it" (Davis, Gardner, and Gardner 1941, quoted in McGovern 1982:6–7).

There is considerable circumstantial evidence to support a hypothesis that the Springfield lynchings were planned and that some of the police and public officials were involved. The conclusion that Coker and Duncan were set up is almost inescapable, and such an interpretation is supported by a 1970 interview by Clary of ninety-four-year-old Daniel Yancey, a black man who witnessed the Springfield lynching. Yancey "asserted that the white community knew that Coker and Duncan were innocent, and that innocent young blacks were purposely chosen as victims in order to terrify the blacks of the city more effectively. He pointed out that to lynch a guilty man would have accomplished little, since thoughtful Negroes would have agreed with the object, if not the method" (Clary 1970:35).

Whatever the differences in their roots and motivations, the end results of the lynchings in the two cities were similar: many blacks were driven out and those who remained were demoralized and subjected to even more severe restrictions than they had experienced in the past. They had been a minority population in both communities and their economic contribution was dispensable. Therefore, whatever the cost in terms of the loss of talented and creative people, the economic losses to Springfield and Joplin were insignificant, and blacks could be debased or driven out with impunity. Today, eighty years later, blacks are very small minorities in Joplin and Springfield with negligible political or economic influence. No black has served on the Springfield city council or the school board since the lynchings. In the most recent school board elections in Springfield (1984), a black candidate ran but finished dead last. The year before, the school board had an unusual opportunity to redress some of the past wrongs done to the black community when two well-qualified blacks joined several white applicants to fill a mid-term vacancy on the board. Instead the board chose a white male professional from an upper-middle-income neighborhood. The legacy of the lynchings has been long and painful indeed and its end is not in sight.

REFERENCES

Brown, Richard Maxwell, 1975. *Strain of Violence* (New York: Oxford University Press).
Clary, Mary N., 1970. The Easter Offering: A Missouri Lynching, 1906. M.A. thesis, Southwest Missouri State University.
Cutler, James E., 1969. *Lynch-law* (Montclair, N.J.: Patterson-Smith).
Davis, Allison, Burleigh B. Gardner, and Mary R. Gardner, 1941. *Deep South: A Social Anthropological Study of Caste and Class* (Chicago: University of Chicago Press).
Egerton, John, 1983. A Case of Prejudice: The Execution of Maurice Mays and the Knoxville Race Riot of 1919. *Southern Exposure* 11(4):56–65.
Flanders, Robert, S. Harris, and D. Quick, 1981. *A Cultural Resources Survey of the Proposed University Plaza Project, City of Springfield, Greene County, Missouri: 1981.* Center for Archaeological Research, Project CAR-441 (Springfield: Southwest Missouri State University).
Grant, Donald L., 1975. *The Anti-Lynching Movement: 1883–1932* (San Francisco: R and E Research Associates).
Greene, Lorenzo J., G. R. Kremer, and A. F. Holland, 1980. *Missouri's Black Heritage* (St. Louis: Forum Press).
Hall, Jacquelyn Dowd, 1979. *Revolt against Chivalry: Jessie Daniel Ames and the Women's Campaign against Lynching* (New York: Columbia University Press).
———, 1984. The Mind that Burns in Each Body: Women, Rape, and Racial Violence. *Southern Exposure* 12(6):61–71.
Harris, Suzanne E., 1981. *An Assessment of Seven Historic Archaeological Sites in the Proposed University Plaza Project Area, City of Springfield, Greene County, Missouri: 1981.* Center for Archaeological Research, Project CAR-481 (Springfield: Southwest Missouri State University).

Howell, Benita J., 1983. The Saga of Jerome Boyatt: A Mirror of Attitudes toward Law and Lawlessness. *Tennessee Anthropologist* 8:1–19.

Lederer, Katherine, 1981a. And Then They Sang a Sabbath Song. *Springfield Magazine* 2(11):26–28, 33–36.

———, 1981b. And Then They Sang a Sabbath Song: Part 3. *Springfield Magazine* 2(12):24–26.

———, 1982. Springfield's Lost Black History: Dedicated to the "Many a Thousand Gone" (A slide lecture and brochure funded by the Missouri Committee for the Humanities).

McGovern, James R., 1982. *Anatomy of a Lynching: The Killing of Claude Neal* (Baton Rouge: Louisiana State University Press).

National Association for the Advancement of Colored People, 1919. *Thirty Years of Lynching in the United States* (New York: Negro University Press).

Ploski, Harry A., and James Williams, eds., 1983. *Negro Almanac* (New York: Wiley-Interscience Publications).

Rafferty, Milton D., 1982. *Historical Atlas of Missouri* (Norman: University of Oklahoma Press).

Raper, Arthur F., 1969. *The Tragedy of Lynching* (New York: Arno Press and the New York Times).

Shaner, Dolph, 1948. *The Story of Joplin* (New York: Stratford House).

U.S. Bureau of the Census, 1904. *Abstract of the Twelfth Census of the United States, 1900* (Washington, D.C.: U.S. Government Printing Office).

White, Walter, 1969. *Rope and Faggot: Biography of Judge Lynch* (New York: Arno Press).

Wood, Forrest G., 1968. *Black Scare: The Racist Response to Emancipation and Reconstruction* (Berkeley: University of California Press).

A Structural Analysis of the Chinese Grocery Store in the Mississippi Delta

Mary Jo Schneider and William M. Schneider

In recent years historians and other scholars have recognized the anomalous phenomenon of the Chinese grocery store in the Delta region of Mississippi and Arkansas. Most outsiders are unaware of their presence in the South, but the Chinese have played an important role in the economy of an area which has been characterized as a caste system of two colors: black and white. Extensive historical accounts exist of the origins and evolution of the Chinese and their grocery stores (Cohen 1984; Tsai 1981; Quan 1982), and Loewen (1971) has developed an impressive socioecological explanation for the phenomenon. This paper aims to add to our understanding of the Chinese grocery by analyzing it according to a cognitive-structural paradigm (Douglas 1966; Lévi-Strauss 1967, 1979; Turner 1974; Van Gennep 1960).

Historically, grocery and community stores have played an important role in the economies of both the plantation and the hill South. During a period when banks were largely absent, both large and small farmers turned to rural stores to supply up to twelve months of credit for groceries and dry goods. Once a year, at the end of the harvest, farmers would pay bills from the proceeds of their crops (Atherton 1949:14). The unusual success of the Chinese grocery and the very high percentage of Chinese in the Delta who are engaged in the grocery trade require a great deal more explanation than is supplied by a simple historical account or even by a sophisticated ecological analysis of the socioeconomic niche occupied by the Chinese grocery. A sufficient understanding of the Chinese grocery requires attention to the cognitive structure of Delta society, or, as Rappaport would put it, the "cognized model" of Delta society (1979) during the past century and the position of the Chinese grocery in that structure. The structural analysis provided by this paper will focus primarily on the Chinese grocery store prior to the time of racial integration.

THE DELTA CHINESE: A BRIEF OVERVIEW

In northwest Mississippi and eastern Arkansas lies a vast alluvial plain, locally known as the Delta. It is an area with a plantation economy, high concentrations of poverty, and scattered small towns. Land is owned mostly by white planters and worked by black as well as by white sharecroppers.

The area was settled mostly after the Civil War. Blacks and whites entered the region together, clearing land, draining the swamps, and erecting shelters. Once land was cleared it was planted in cotton. An economy evolved dependent on large landholdings and black and white farm laborers working on a furnish-sharecrop system. Until about 1950 most work related to growing cotton was done by hand. Agricultural mechanization ended this system and resulted in a heavy migration of rural blacks and whites.

During Reconstruction (1866–1876), there was a substantial need for labor in the Delta to do the work necessary for agricultural production. Blacks were brought in from surrounding areas, but blacks, who could now vote, were viewed with suspicion. Planters' associations made an effort to obtain northerners and European immigrants without much success. Day wages were paid to local blacks and whites, but labor was in short supply. Chinese, who were known as successful workers in the Caribbean and the western United States, seemed to be a solution.

Chinese were believed to be docile, and the political rights of citizens did not have to be awarded to them. Chinese workers entered into labor contracts with planters and managers. At first, according to newspaper accounts, the Chinese were viewed extremely positively. The Chinese were praised for their high-quality work, their dedication, their cleanliness, and their quiet nature. However, this positive view was soon tempered as disputes arose between the Chinese and their employers over the terms of the labor contracts. Planters who had been used to virtually absolute control over their slaves now found their authority questioned. Rebellions, work stoppages, court suits, and desertion were some of the techniques that the Chinese used to defend themselves against what they viewed as unfair labor practices. Planters found that the courts rarely enforced the contractual obligations of Chinese workers.

The experiment with Chinese agricultural labor soon ended. The Chinese had been expensive to import. They did not make especially good farmhands. And, perhaps most important, by 1876 the political power and social rights of blacks had been curbed and power was firmly again in the hands of whites. Sharecropping replaced day labor. It was more economically profitable and less confusing.

Most Chinese did not stay to work as sharecroppers but left the cotton fields to become peddlers or merchants (small grocers) and over the ensuing decades they rapidly enhanced their economic and social position. Chinese were considered neither black nor white. The Chinese were viewed to be members of an ancient though heathen civilization (Cohen 1984:32). The prevalent stereotype of the Chinese largely lacked the alleged biological and mental inferiority attributed to blacks. Chinese were viewed as clannish, cunning, and crafty. An 1880 Louisiana census shows that Chinese men were married to black, mulatto, Chinese, and white women.

The special status of the Chinese was demonstrated by the triply segregated school systems of some Mississippi towns in the 1930s and 1940s. Since the 1940s, the Chinese have attended the white public schools and have been admitted into other traditionally white institutions. In most respects, the Delta Chinese today are nearly equal to whites in social status. Ethnic markers such as arranged marriages, celebrations of the Chinese New Year, and speaking Chinese in the home still separate Chinese from other white Southerners. But the two groups intermarry and college-age Chinese young people say they experienced no discrimination in their hometowns because of their ethnic heritage.

The first Chinese men to move to the Delta were not true immigrants but sojourners planning to return to China. The villages of southern China had a tradition of sending young men out to all areas of the world to add to the family estate. On a return visit, a man would take a bride who might or might not accompany him when he left again. The goal was to work, send money home, and retire to China a wealthy man who could be buried in Chinese soil. Delta Chinese fit much the same ecological niche in Mississippi and Arkansas as they did and do elsewhere in the world. Chinese grocery stores that look much like those in the Delta are found from Costa Rica to Borneo.

In the earlier years, some Chinese men married blacks or took black common-law wives (some were married to women left in China as well), but as the Chinese moved up in the social hierarchy they saw that black-Chinese marriages were clearly against their best interests and pressured other Chinese against such alliances. Today, white-Chinese marriages sometimes occur. Typically, Chinese men marry into the working-class ranks. Chinese may date whites, but both sets of parents are likely to disapprove of what they consider to be interracial marriages.

Chinese-white high school social patterns vary widely. Our informants were University of Arkansas students from Delta communities in eastern and southern Arkansas. In some communities Chinese appear to date other Chinese exclusively and to have mostly Chinese friends. In other communities there is much more socializing between Chinese and white young people. Some Chinese students seem to be well accepted by whites, while others are excluded from white friendship cliques. Patterns of white acceptance seem to be related to degree of assimilation or Americanization. Parents of Chinese teenagers exert a great deal of control over their children's activities. Some prohibit dating, and all seem to expect stellar school performance as well as help with the family business.

In the Delta today, a social and economic gap remains between the dominant white and the subordinate black groups. In some communities the Chinese bridge the color gap, standing as an intermediate group. They are both privileged and burdened with an ambiguous racial identity. In the past this ambiguous racial identity was even more marked, but as cultural distinctiveness lessens the Chinese appear to be gradually moving toward a white racial identity.

BEGINNINGS

By the early 1870s, Chinese grocery stores were beginning to appear in the Delta. The early Chinese store was no more than a shack, measuring perhaps twenty by twenty feet. Chinese merchants and their families generally lived in the back of their stores. Living in the rear of the store reduced costs, prevented much thievery, and avoided the caste prescriptions for residential segregation.

Planters typically operated commissaries which supplied goods to sharecroppers on credit with high interest charges, sometimes reaching 100 percent annually. At the end of the harvest season, the sharecropper's bill was subtracted from the price awarded for the crop. But as demand for increased agricultural labor developed, many plantation owners got out of the commissary business, leaving a niche for an entrepreneur. The early Chinese groceries, like the plantation commissaries they replaced, carried only staples—meat, meal, and molasses—and they offered credit to their customers. Chinese grocers prospered through their frugality and hard work.

Grocery stores were, and are, generally located in black neighborhoods, and except for the more modern and expanded stores which have been built in larger towns in recent years, most look weather-beaten and dilapidated. Quan (1982:13) says that older Chinese hesitate to live too luxuriously because of the resentment they fear from blacks and whites. Old commercial signs, large thermometers, and calendars, along with packed shelves, contribute to the stores' ambience.

Why did the grocery store appear? Chinese were oriented toward economic success, and sharecropping did not offer much hope of material reward. Moreover, after Reconstruction ended planters preferred black to Oriental labor. Chinese in the Delta did not face a wide variety of economic options. Chinese in other parts of the country were opening laundries or becoming domestics, but in these roles Chinese would compete directly with blacks for substandard wages in the Delta. Blacks had little money to spend for anything except clothing and food, and the few whites had little discretionary income. Young Chinese had extremely limited capital, but a small investment was sufficient to rent a tiny store building and sell groceries from the front room while living in the back. The clientele consisted almost entirely of poor blacks who worked on nearby plantations or at menial jobs in town. Operating a grocery store in the Delta was not an easy road to riches. Low working capital and the necessity to send money back to China combined with limited credit from suppliers allowed the Chinese storekeeper to keep only a small inventory of rapid turnover items. Profit margins were high, but provision of credit to customers was both essential and risky. Chinese grocers were largely without legal recourse to prosecute thieves or those who did not pay bills. Despite these problems, Chinese grocers were remarkably successful.

Kin ties among Chinese grocers helped to establish good reputations among creditors. Wholesalers knew that any losses would be made up either by the grocer's relatives or by other Chinese merchants who feared that their own reputations would be tarnished by the delinquent accounts of another Chinese businessman. When businesses became profitable, merchants would send for relatives in China who would work first as apprentices and then begin to operate their own stores. For this reason there are many kin ties among the Delta Chinese.

The values of neither Delta blacks nor whites sanctioned hard work and commercial enterprise, but among the Chinese the ideal of an independent business was cherished. While local blacks might have difficulty collecting debts from relatives and friends, the Chinese as outsiders had few such personal obligations. Nor were Chinese bound by the pervasive caste etiquette which considered waiting on customers to be less than an honorable way to make a living.

The ecological niche occupied by the Chinese in the Delta was similar to that held by Jewish merchants in both small and large communities in the South. Jews, like Chinese, shared ethnic traditions which held retail trade to be respectable. Like the Chinese, Jews were outsiders who differed from their Gentile neighbors in religion, occupation, and racial attitude.

A STRUCTURAL ANALYSIS

In the last three decades French anthropologist Claude Lévi-Strauss has become a major figure in both European and American anthropology. Lévi-Strauss advocates an approach to social and cultural data known as the structural method of analysis. Structural analysis aims at uncovering cultural themes, relationships, and connections rather than at developing scientific laws.

In Lévi-Strauss' method, cultures divide themselves into organic entities so that society as a whole can be integrated or unified. Unity or solidarity comes from patterns of exchange among groups. Thus, Delta society with its all-pervasive binary caste structure is to be understood in terms of the exchange relations between its constituent parts, blacks and whites. Lévi-Strauss writes, "exchange in human society is a universal means of ensuring the interlocking of its constituent parts and that this exchange can operate at different levels among which the more important are food, goods and services, and women" (1979:143).

Lévi-Strauss (1967) also demonstrates the importance of what he considers to be the universal human drive to classify the world, to break up the chaotic continua that exist in nature into orderly categories which he believes, at bottom, are binary opposites. Humans, thereby, impose cultural order on chaotic nature. The black-white binary contrast is a crucial opposition in the Delta.

Other thinkers writing in the same vein have dealt with related issues which inform our understanding of the Chinese grocery in the Delta. Arnold Van Gennep (1960) and Victor Turner (1969) argue that mediating categories are liminal and therefore partake of a very special, sacred character, either positive or negative. In his book, *The Ritual Process* (1969), Turner writes about structure, antistructure, and *communitas*. Turner concerns himself most particularly with the liminal in human experience. Liminality describes the transitional quality of beings, objects, phases, and so forth that are "betwixt and between" categories of human classification. Turner and Mary Douglas (1966) show us that mediating categories are always problematic and are therefore tabooed because they do not fit in with the prevailing system of classification. Turner further points out the special bond and quality of interaction that exist among members of a group that are together in a liminal position. *Communitas* is the washing out of hierarchical distinctions among members of a liminal group, such as a group of initiates in a rite of passage. All of these writers lead us to expect special qualities to be associated with the Chinese grocers in the minds of both blacks and whites in the Delta. These cognitive qualities are not necessarily the same as social reality, but they are nonetheless very powerful determinants of human behavior. People can only act in terms of the reality which they perceive. While "white" is associated with power, wealth, goodness, civilization, and culture, "black" symbolizes its opposites: subordination, poverty, evil, barbarism, and nature.

The black/white contrast pervades every aspect of Delta life and social structure. Those who are neither black nor white pose a cognitive structural problem, but in their problematic character they allow solutions to the inherent social structural problems of the caste structure. They are in limbo, but they may mediate between binary poles of black and white. People of mixed black and white ancestry may not serve as mediators since they are automatically classed with the subordinate group.

The Chinese formed a mediating category because, being new to the sociocultural system, they were forced into neither polar category. Being neither black nor white, and making little or no attempt, at least at first, to be categorized as either, the Chinese could mediate between the two caste groups without becoming a part of either. The Chinese permitted communication and exchange between blacks and whites while maintaining their separation. In a sense, the Chinese allowed the system of segregation to be perpetuated by being the mediating category between the bipolar extremes. Because the Chinese merchant existed, blacks did not enter "inappropriate" occupations. Whites did not need to lower their status by becoming merchants to blacks.

The structuralist approach throws into stark relief the Chinese grocery store in Delta society. The grocery store is, after all, a mechanism of exchange, principally for food and other goods, but also for services and information between blacks and whites. This exchange would be more difficult without the brokerage provided by the grocer. The Chinese grocer handles the powerfully degrading commercial transactions between neighbor and kin, black and white, while the store becomes a liminal arena for the exchange of information and the negotiation of service contracts between blacks and whites. If the grocer were either black or white, the grocer could not mediate as effectively between black and white castes since confusion about proper role behavior would occur. Either a black or a white grocer would lose social standing as a result of engaging in small retail trade, for violating norms of proper behavior to neighbor and kin, and by doing manual labor. The white grocer loses social rank because of polluting dealings with black customers. But the ethnic Chinese was the perfect grocer for the Delta prior to the Civil Rights movement.

Through the grocery store, blacks gained access to products of white society otherwise unavailable to them. Blacks needed the products and the credit terms Chinese merchants provided. A peripheral person from the margins of the system is the ideal mediator between opposed parts of the system. (Compare the Nuer leopard-skin chief or the Kalinga *monkalun* in feud situations.) The outsider does not embarrass the structure, as would either a black or white mediator. Marginal ethnics thus become essential to maintaining the social system of which they do not consider themselves to be a part.

According to traditional Delta values, retail trade itself—the buying and selling of many inexpensive items that involves a person in a large number of small commercial transactions motivated by the desire for profit at the expense of neighbors—is a questionable activity. It contradicts important values of neighborliness, kin obligation, and white *noblesse oblige*. One may make large trades at a profit and be admired so long as the trading partner is not too close a member of the social system. One may perform professional services for others (so long as they do not involve violations of pollution taboos like cross-racial barbering and undertaking) and be seen as rendering a desired and needed activity. But constant profiteering at the expense of neighbors and kin and the frequent conflicts resulting from bill collection in the community present the would-be small merchant with a choice between social status and money profit. In the Delta society, profit interests were secondary to needs for maintaining and improving social status for most blacks and whites.

The Chinese grocer and grocery are simultaneously at the heart of and on the margins of Delta society, conceptually outside of the system while fundamentally integral to the flow of goods, services, and information. But the Chinese grocer as a marginal person poses a difficult cognitive problem for the principal participants in the Delta social system. We will follow Turner in employing the term "liminal" to describe the in-between character of the Chinese grocer. Liminal beings, things, or phases are ritually very highly charged and explicitly set apart from the rest of the society. The shaman who moves between the worlds of the natural and the supernatural; the sacred virgin hovering between childhood and motherhood; the church mediating between heaven and earth; and the graveyard (particularly at midnight), the threshold between the living and dead, are all examples of liminal beings or places. This part of the theory would predict that the Chinese grocer and grocery would be considered highly charged, sacred, or magical in some respects.

Let us now examine the data available to us from black and white informants from the Delta. The primary clientele of the grocery seems to be an important determinant of the local image of the Chinese grocer. In those communities where the Chinese served substantial numbers of whites, the Chinese tended to be viewed as fascinating, charming, and the source of hidden wisdom. As one middle-aged former Delta resident told us, when he was a child he believed that the Chinese in his community were the source of hidden wisdom. They were the inscrutable Orientals with wisdom Caucasians lacked. He speculated that they could cast spells and practiced some sort of Buddhism. As a ten-year-old boy, a trip to the Chinese grocery was like a trip to Disneyworld—it was a bit scary, but not threatening. Another former eastern Arkansas male remembered the Chinese as "smart—smart as the devil."

Our students from Delta communities where Chinese served mostly blacks say that even today some middle-class whites avoid contact with Chinese grocers, considering their stores off-limits. As one young man from southern Arkansas told us, "You never see the same dog twice lying around a Chinese grocery store. I never go near the place." A young white woman from Pine Bluff confirmed that she would be most uncomfortable entering the neighborhood Chinese grocery store in her hometown. A middle-aged woman from an aristocratic Dumas, Arkansas family confided that her father's friends were hesitant to associate with the Chinese and viewed them with "contempt." In this community, Chinese merchants had mostly black customers. Predictably, those counties where many Chinese grocery stores remain are the most segregated today.

Chinese place of residence differs according to the two types of communities. Where Chinese serve mostly black customers, they tend to live in or on the margins of the black community; where their customers are largely white, Chinese tend to live on the outskirts of the white community. In Blytheville, Arkansas, for example, the Chinese customarily live on the edge of the white section of town toward the farming area—a liminal place of residence. In Stuttgart, Chinese grocers live on the margins of the black community—in the black portion of town, but very near the white section. In Marianna, where some Chinese families resided in a middle-class white section of town, one white neighbor of a Chinese family erected a high fence on the property line. Blacks with whom we have spoken view the Chinese as more like whites than like blacks. They speak of present-day liaisons between Chinese and blacks, backstreet romances which cannot be revealed.

To blacks, the Chinese represent a needed group—people who can extend credit and provide essential services. Blacks view Chinese as materialistic, rich, and exploitive. They comment, as do whites, on the extreme formality and propriety of Chinese merchants. My informants describe Chinese merchants as "aloof, distant, and clannish." They may be speaking Chinese when a customer enters the store, but stop immediately. One dreams of the Chinese who practice some old and mysteriously efficacious, exotic religion, but on Sunday morning the Chinese may participate in the local Baptist or Methodist Church and may even tell co-worshipers about the success of Christian missionary efforts in the old country. Young Chinese informants do not seem to want to believe that their ethnicity is especially interesting or important. Although some come from homes where one or both parents speak Chinese, there appears to be little attempt to pass on the language or Chinese customs and traditions to children.

Turner, in concentrating on the special character of liminality, examines the antistructural aspect of liminality or what he calls the quality of *communitas*. A liminal structural position frequently involves a radical shift in the structural order of ordinary conditions. Sometimes this is manifested as a complete reversal of social hierarchy, so that a king may be treated as a commoner and vice-versa, or perhaps simply an erasure of hierarchical social distinctions may occur, as, for example, during initiation rites when all initiates occupy the same structural position. This part of the theory suggests that the Chinese grocer would have no social rank in a highly hierarchical society. In fact, it is this very absence of an assigned social rank that allows the Chinese to serve a brokerage function. They are unencumbered by caste etiquette. Thus they are not shamed by "waiting on" either blacks or whites. As a liminal group, as middlemen, the Chinese performed essential services for their clientele. Blacks who had difficulty obtaining money might approach Chinese grocers for loans, bond money, or credit. Both blacks and whites might receive assistance from Chinese grocers with Social Security forms and letters. These brokerage services may have helped to maintain traditional social relations between blacks and whites. Here appears a seeming contradiction: while the Chinese grocery store and the Chinese ethnic group in general by their very existence maintained the traditional order of segregation, the grocery store as a liminal place, a place of *communitas,* was the place where social hierarchies were least apparent of any Delta institution. Mediation functions continue today. In one small eastern Arkansas community, a Chinese man today serves as mayor. In this position, he mediates successfully between whites and blacks. One young Chinese woman told us that she feels that blacks trust Chinese more than they trust whites since Chinese share none of the legacy of slavery and racial exclusion that are a part of the southern burden for both whites and blacks.

Both blacks and whites were treated with formality by the Chinese merchant. In the early days, Chinese merchants spoke little English, and customers used pointer sticks to identify the goods they wanted. Even during the past two decades our observations recorded little polite chit-chat between Chinese grocers and their customers. While Brer Rabbit talked of the etiquette-ridden South where everyone was obliged to ask after family, where indirectness and discretion were a way of life, these codes of etiquette were largely ignored by the Chinese grocer. The Chinese merchant treats blacks and whites similarly. The store is a place for economic transactions between merchant and customer and for some social exchange. The situation approaches *communitas:* caste and class distinctions are minimized, although not eliminated, and the rules of caste and class etiquette which are applied in other settings are not found in the Chinese grocery store. Belonging to a liminal category, the Chinese were free to (or obligated to) ignore the prevalent value system which frowned on manual labor, and making a profit on one's neighbors, and emphasized social position.

The Chinese seem to be aware of the advantages of being liminal and contributing to both black and white political causes and conflicting charities as a way of maintaining their "betwixt and between" position. Chinese grocery stores with predominantly black clientele provided more opportunity for *communitas* than those with mostly white customers. Whites could always enter a business blacks frequented, while stores serving mostly whites inhibited blacks from entering or at least from lingering. The grocery store was often a liminal place, where *communitas* was approached. But *communitas* was not complete. Whites and blacks tended to sit at separate tables while they enjoyed a beer and a smoke. Black men and white men might linger together outside the store, "vertically integrated" (in Delta phraseology) because they were hunkering or standing instead of sitting. The Chinese grocery store stands as an important mediating force in the Mississippi Delta, a traditionally polarized society where traditions kept blacks and whites apart. The Chinese, a liminal group, helped to maintain caste structure, fitting into an ecological niche that neither blacks nor whites viewed as culturally desirable although it was economically profitable. In some communities, the Chinese grocery store served as a place of *communitas* where caste distinctions became minimized. As Delta Chinese become more acculturated and higher in economic status and as caste distinctions between blacks and whites in the region disappear, the liminality of the Chinese largely will disappear also.

The Chinese grocery store in the Delta is in sharp contrast with country stores in the hill South, which largely lacks the ethnic diversity and the marked social class stratification so characteristic of the plantation South. In the overwhelmingly white hill South, the social standing of the storekeeper and the social functions of the grocery store are far different from those described in this paper. In rural Appalachian and Ozark communities in the past, stores and storekeepers provided the main avenue of communication with the outside world. Prior to World War II the hill storekeeper stood at the apex of the social order. Far more than either churches or schools, stores served as daily arenas of social activity and provided goods from the outside.

Storeowners in the more egalitarian South might pass on information about livestock sales or other community events, and they would deliver messages to customers. A stranger might seek information at the store, and residents might go to the store to sign up for a government program. By visiting the store a resident would learn of births, deaths, illnesses, fires, and thefts.

In contrast with the Chinese storekeepers, who exchanged little information and gossip with their customers, Ozark and Appalachian storekeepers used information as a commodity that could attract customers to their stores (Hicks 1976). Storekeepers had to be skilled gossipers—knowing what to tell and what to keep secret. Storekeepers might prevent an arrest by refusing to divulge the whereabouts of community residents to outsiders, and they probably attempted to promote marital harmony by selective disclosure of information as well.

Whereas the hill South storekeeper's survival in part depended on adept social skills and diplomatic refusal to extend too much credit, the Chinese storekeeper largely was uninvolved in community affairs and personal diplomacy. A hill store might be patronized because of friendly gestures on the part of the storekeeper, but the Chinese store was patronized in a spirit of neutrality and for lack of better alternatives. The Chinese grocer remained reasonably aloof from community politics.

The typical Chinese-owned grocery store was probably more profitable than those owned by either whites or blacks. The neutral Chinese could refuse credit without being subjected to the harsh criticism that a kinsman or neighbor might fall victim to. And when the profits of a hill storekeeper became sizable, competing stores were likely to arise. Not so in the Delta, where caste etiquette and cultural rules devalued the storekeeper whose customers were primarily black. The Chinese grocer was freer to operate a business for profit and to refuse to perform unprofitable neighborly services such as free use of tools and the telephone.

REFERENCES

Atherton, Lewis F., 1949. *The Southern Country Store, 1830–1860* (Baton Rouge: Louisiana State University Press).

Cohen, Lucy, 1984. *Chinese in the Post–Civil War South* (Baton Rouge: Louisiana State University Press).

Douglas, Mary, 1966. *Purity and Danger* (Middlesex: Penguin).

Hicks, George, 1976. *Appalachian Valley* (New York: Holt, Rinehart and Winston).

Lévi-Strauss, Claude, 1979. The Bear and the Barber. In *Reader in Comparative Religion*, 4th ed., William A. Lessa and Evon Z. Vogt, eds. (New York: Harper and Row), pp. 141–148.

————, 1967. *Structural Anthropology* (New York: Doubleday).

Loewen, James, 1971. *The Mississippi Chinese* (Cambridge, Mass.: Harvard University Press).

Quan, Robert Seto, 1982. *Lotus among the Magnolias* (Jackson: University of Mississippi Press).

Rappaport, Roy, 1979. *Ecology, Meaning, and Religion* (Richmond, Calif.: North Atlantic Books).

Tsai, Shin-shan Henry, 1981. *The Chinese in Arkansas* (final report prepared for the Arkansas Endowment for the Humanities).

Turner, Victor, 1969. *The Ritual Process* (Harmondsworth, England: Penguin).

Van Gennep, A. L., 1960 (orig. 1909). *The Rites of Passage.* M. B. Vizedom and G. L. Cafee, trans. (Chicago: University of Chicago Press).

From Memories and from the Ground: Historical Archeology at the Moser Farmstead in the Arkansas Ozarks

Leslie C. Stewart-Abernathy

A recent collection of folk beliefs and practices begins with the following comments: "the epitome of the bittersweet life seems to be the Ozarks. Over a hundred and fifty years ago, ambitious family groups . . . populated the country and established a way of life which did not change much until the 1940s . . . isolated to a degree for over a hundred years, they continued their predominantly rural way of life longer than most of the rest of America" (Massey 1978:xi–xiii, 1–3). This is not an uncommon collection of sentiments, for the Ozarks region of northern Arkansas and southern Missouri is often considered in our national culture as a unique place with a special way of life, a special history of continuity, and a special tradition.

The survival of this image—what might be called the Ozark Tradition Myth—is not surprising given the drastically altered landscape and demography of the New Ozarks (Rafferty 1980). Thousands of Ozarkers fled the uplands in the four decades after 1900, some heading to regional urban centers and others moving as far away as California. An enormous system of recreational lakes was built by the U.S. Army Corps of Engineers in the 1940s and 1950s, drowning hundreds of thousands of acres containing thousands of farmsteads and hundreds of villages and hamlets. These lakes have drawn in new population in the form of enormous numbers of tourists and retirees. Retirees have come in enough numbers to shift the demographic profile of the entire state. In the late twentieth century the Ozark Tradition Myth is the only image of the past most people can find in many places in the Ozarks.

The Ozark Tradition Myth provides a substantial part of the base upon which a multimillion-dollar tourist and craft industry has been built. However, the myth is intriguing because it celebrates contradictory values: self-reliance and poverty; family strength and familial incest; spiritual stamina and crippling superstition; hardy pioneers amidst industrialization and ignorant hicks; cleverness in the face of lowlander schemes and helplessness in the face of outsider predation. The negative aspects of this Ozark image support hillbilly stereotypes. Snuffy Smith is considered by many to be the image of an Ozarker, although Al Capp set Dogpatch in Appalachia. The positive aspects, on the other hand, provide a valued yeoman rural heritage for the urbanized third- and fourth-generation descendants of Ozark pioneers (see Harington 1975). For many contemporary Ozark residents the myth provides their livelihoods by luring tourists and retirees. Thus Dogpatch has become incarnate as a tourist attraction near Harrison in Boone County, Arkansas. The Ozark "way of life," in both its positive and negative aspects, has been reported in constant danger of extinction since at least 1925, but this only adds piquancy and urgency to travel brochures, allowing promoters to exploit the voyeurism of a culture in its death throes.

The contradictions in the Ozark Tradition Myth are inviting because they direct our attention to significant problems which can reveal a great deal about the nature of traditional Ozark lifeways.

In order to evaluate the contradictions in the Ozark Tradition Myth, it is necessary first to understand the actual lifeways and history upon which the myth is based. Modern scholars have found much valuable information on Ozark lifeways collected by folklore writers such as Vance Randolph (Cochran and Luster 1979), Otto W. Rayburn (1941), and others less well known who were at work in the 1920s to 1940s. The popular works of these writers, however, contributed to the formation of the myth and few would claim that these accounts provide the whole story. Useful but also incomplete are memoirs of native Ozarkers (Page 1977; Wolf 1974). Historical archeology (Deetz 1977; Schuyler 1978) provides an alternative approach to evaluating the Ozark Tradition Myth. The routines of past Ozark daily life to which the myth refers survive as documents in archives and as artifacts and soil stains in the ground. When these data are combined with ethnographic details elicited from living informants, historical archeologists are able to explore contradictions in the Ozark Tradition Myth using both etic and emic perspectives.

An opportunity for this kind of study came with the proposed realignment of a major highway, U.S. 71, through the western margin of the Arkansas Ozarks. The new route for this highway in central Benton County was laid directly through the remains of a historic farmstead site (Figure 1) discovered during a preliminary archeological survey. The Moser site, as it came to be known, was home to two generations of farm families between its initial beginnings about 1875 and its final abandonment in 1919. After the demolition of the farmstead in the 1920s and 1930s, the existence of the place was generally forgotten.

Federal laws require that when significant cultural resources are endangered by federally supported projects, steps must be taken to either protect the resource (in this case an archeological site) or to conduct intensive research to recover the significant cultural data (King, Hickman, and Berg 1977). Until the Moser site was discovered, there had not been an intensive examination of a similar site in the Arkansas Ozarks dating to the late 1800s or early 1900s. Excavations in the eastern Ozarks of Missouri (Price and Price 1978) and also in the Cypress Creek basin (Santeford, Martin, and Hemmings 1985) had demonstrated, however, that historic farmstead sites can indeed provide valuable cultural data. The Moser site was consequently determined to be significant within the guidelines established for historic sites in the Arkansas state plan for the conservation of archeological resources (Davis 1982; Stewart-Abernathy and Watkins 1982).

Protection of the Moser farmstead site (3BE311) was not possible, so in 1983 excavations were conducted at the site by the Arkansas Archeological Survey under contract with the Arkansas Highway and Transportation Department and the Federal Highway Administration (Stewart-Abernathy 1985). These excavations produced abundant data pertinent to a critical examination of major themes comprising the Ozark Tradition Myth. Protected deposits of ordinary household trash provided evidence of the little-remembered, tangible accoutrements of daily routine discarded at the end of practical or symbolic utility. Over fifteen thousand artifacts were found at the site in five protected deposits. In addition to the archeological data legal and commercial documents were examined for information on the chronological and geo-

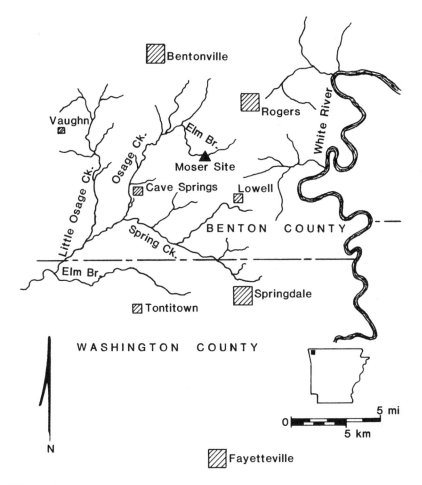

Figure 1
The Moser Farmstead Site, 3BE311. (After Figure 1-1, Stewart-Abernathy 1985.)

graphic contexts of the site. Finally, living informants gave us the remembered experiences of participation in past behavior at the farmstead site. Particularly useful to this study was information gained from Mr. Dallas Moser, who lived at the farmstead from 1907 to 1915, and Mr. Sid Chastain, a neighbor and childhood friend of Mr. Moser who helped demolish the farmstead after the last inhabitants left in 1919. These informants provided details that aided the archeological research and also details about aspects of behavior that left little visible record. None of these three data sets were complete by themselves, and in some cases they did not even overlap. But when these data sets are integrated intimate views of farmstead routines are revealed which eighty years later appear neither routine nor familiar.

The Moser data will be used here to discuss one major theme of the Ozark Tradition Myth. Much of the myth is based on the notion that families in the Ozark uplands were economically independent. The Moser data provide a context for evaluating the meaning of economic independence in at least this one circumstance. Although the complete range of lifeways in the region is not reflected by the Moser data, basic patterns revealed at this site must be incorporated into the Ozark story. This examination of the independence theme also provides one example of the kinds of insight regarding aspects of the myth that can be derived from archeological research enlivened by ethnohistory.

THE NATURE OF ECONOMIC INDEPENDENCE AT THE MOSER FARMSTEAD

One basic pattern suggested at the Moser farmstead was that its inhabitants clearly strived for economic independence. By looking at a reconstructed plan of the farmstead and buildings, we can see a strong commitment to a strategy of self-sufficiency based on the family. They took a great deal of responsibility for production and maintenance of the goods and services necessary to making a living and providing a home. The base line for the reconstruction is 1910, from oral data available in great detail for the occupation of the Jeff and Rosy Moser family, including son Dallas Moser. This base line is extended back by supplemental archeological data. It might be noted that in spite of decades of outsider observation of Ozark lifeways, there are only a handful of careful reconstructions of farmsteads available.

The Moser farmstead sat on the edge of a low bluff above the floodplain of a small stream known to the families as Elm Branch. The stead, about 2.5 acres (1 hectare), was shaped like a halfmoon or horseshoe with the open end on a draw that led down to the foot of the bluff (Figure 2). The farmstead included a variety of buildings and spaces designed to support a way of life based on mixed husbandry.

The house, built about 1880, was one story, frame, and had seven rooms organized with a traditional central hall plan and a kitchen ell. Higher architectural intentions for the building are perhaps suggested by the fact that the central hall was never an open dogtrot, and the symmetrical front facade was highlighted with a small gabled portico at the front door. By 1910 the house was equipped with a fireplace for heat and a woodstove connected through a blocked fireplace for kitchen use. A brick cistern equipped with a water filtration basin was conveniently located under the kitchen ell porch. Beneath this ell was a shallow storage cellar, dug out about 1895. The cellar was reached by an outside door.

Within the house yard was a log smokehouse, the only log building on the stead after 1900. Under this structure was another small storage cellar, dug out sometime before 1890. This cellar was apparently the first on the farmstead but was abandoned and filled with trash when the larger kitchen cellar was dug. The only other obvious feature within the yard fence, aside from decorative plantings and numerous trees to provide shade and block the wind, was a roughly built earthen storm cellar dug about 1913 after a tornado struck nearby. Though the storm cellar was convenient to the back porch of the house, it was seldom used for anything and was eventually filled with trash and allowed to collapse.

Other farmstead elements included two frame chicken houses and a seldom-used privy northeast of the house on the edge of the bluff. A barn stood in the far northwest corner of the farmstead, also on the bluff edge. Milk cows were kept and mules and horses raised for use on the farm and for sale. Inside the barn was also another granary. A cow lot was attached to the barn on the protected south side. South of this lot and west of the house was an enormous garden, with one corner given over seasonally to food storage pits. A hog pasture east of the house and a separate hog feeder lot west of the house provided controlled space for wandering sows and market hogs. Across the road and southwest of the house was a large wagon barn. Finally, there was a

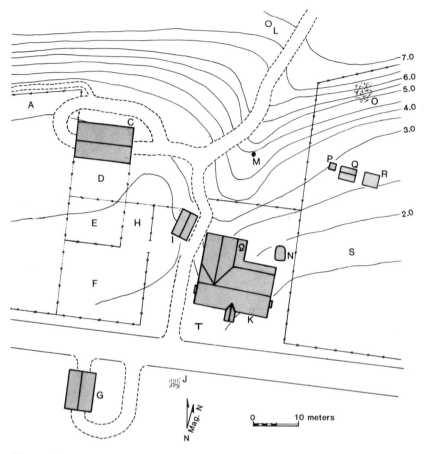

Figure 2

Reconstructed Moser Farmstead Plan, circa 1910. A, stackyard; B, cane/
millet field; C, barn; D, cow lot; E, hog lot; F, garden; G, wagon
shed; H, vegetable "hills"; I, smokehouse; J, firewood pile; K, house;
L, well; M, hog scalding area vicinity walnut tree; N, storm cellar;
O, erosional cuts filled by conscious disposal of household trash;
P, privy; Q–R, chicken houses; S, hog pasture; T, door yard with
perennial flowers along road and front of house. (After Figure 11-1,
Stewart-Abernathy 1985.)

dug well, somewhat inconveniently located down at the foot of the bluff below the house. Unfortunately, it was also downhill from the livestock and chicken areas.

From this farmstead the inhabitants operated an eighty-acre farm that included all the necessary land types, including a field in the creek bottom for rowcrops, upland and bottom land pasture, a wood lot, and space given to a small apple orchard.

The Moser site inhabitants did not confine themselves to primitive agricultural techniques but operated their farm by practices largely standard throughout the South and much of the agricultural United States. No cotton or great fields of wheat were grown, so the distinctive labor and technology for those crops were absent. Other appropriate technologies were available and utilized. For example, mule-drawn implements at the farmstead in the decade before World War I included factory-made plows with shares specially designed for rocky soils, cultivators, planters, and mowers and rakes for hay. Informant Dallas Moser reported that when it came to processing the small crops of millet, wheat, and other small grains grown for use on the farm they did not use a flail. Instead, they employed the services of a massive steam-powered thresher with crew that came through the neighborhood during harvest season. Any variations in equipment, practice, or seasonality that occurred were apparently only those expected for variations in crops, soils, and climate.

From this farm the Moser families obtained most of the meat, grain, and vegetables consumed by themselves and their animals and all of their water and firewood. They preserved many of their garden vegetables and some of the meat through canning. They made their own butter and sauerkraut and used the kitchen ell cellar to provide a stable environment in which to process and protect these and other foodstuffs. They butchered hogs for home use and smoked the hams. And they made sure of keeping good neighbors honest by locking that smoked meat in the smokehouse, the only building on the farmstead with a door that was kept locked.

The analysis so far suggests the Moser families succeeded at maintaining economic self-sufficiency. However, their independence was far from complete. They were in fact another element in a worldwide system of exchange, whether or not they realized the full dimensions of that exchange. Their independence was limited, because through

choice and by necessity they sought and acquired some of the goods
and foodstuffs that world trade and industrialization made available. To
gain access to those items they sent out their agricultural products to
feed the factory workers and other producers and to provide the needed
raw materials.

Such integration with wider economic patterns should be no surprise, but the Ozark Tradition Myth prevents us from seeing certain
obvious situations in which independence is severely restricted. For
example, in the Ozark Tradition Myth, coffee is often cited, perhaps
apologetically, as one of the few exotic products that had to be brought
to the farmstead. This quick mention does not do justice to the incredi-
ble commercial organization that brought the coffee from thousands of
miles away, nor does it hint at the implications of technology and reci-
procity demanded by the simple cup of coffee. Rosy Moser bought her
coffee as beans, but she ground them in a factory-made coffee grinder
similar to the ones frequently exhibited in quaint photos of Ozark interiors. The ceramic or metal cup from which the coffee was drunk came
from outside the farmstead, as did the coffeepot, the cast iron stove on
which the coffee was boiled, the stove pipe, and the axeheads, wedges,
and sawblades used to cut the firewood to fuel the stove. Based on
Moser oral data, also coming in from outside factories were the table
and chairs, the ceramic sugar bowl and cream pitcher, the stirring
spoon, and even the fabric, buttons, needle, and thread Rosy used to
make the apron she wore to protect her clothing from the sooty stove
and the boiling coffeepot.

Part of the direct evidence for Moser family participation in these
broad-scale exchange networks is emic. Oral data strongly emphasize
the fact that these people knew much about the wider world. For example, aside from the milk cows, mule teams, a couple of saddle horses,
and some meat hogs, most of the four-footed stock was raised specifically for sale. Hogs were sold to butchers in nearby towns, and mules
were shipped out by middlemen to the Midwest and South via the
railroad. Much of the arable land was devoted to corn to feed livestock
for market. As informant Dallas Moser put is succinctly, although his
mother Rosy kept 150 to 200 hens, "we didn't have any surplus eggs."
The hens were kept primarily to produce eggs and chicken carcasses
for the market. In short, instead of being subsistence farmers who ate
their crops and sold a bit on the side, the Moser family was closely

involved in production deliberately for the market. This activity involved a great deal of long-term planning rather than just taking advantage of the disposal of fortuitous surpluses.

We are not dependent only on emic perspectives transmitted through memory to show the connections and the implied dependence. The analysis of artifacts from the historical archeological record can also be revealing on matters of which site inhabitants themselves may not have been aware. People acquire, use, and eventually discard or lose the objects that are later found shattered as artifacts. Decades later, participant-informants may find those same objects barely recognizable. They may be able to make functional identifications of some specimens and clarify critical contexts of use, but in the absence of vivid associations the specific details of acquisition and discard are often not remembered. However, standard analysis of two kinds on the artifacts themselves is useful in revealing outside contact. One is an examination of manufacturers' marks; the other is a search for sets.

By the end of the 1800s the industrial system had been churning out products for over a century. Many of those products were provided with manufacturers' marks that can be studied to determine who produced the object, where it was produced, and often approximately when it was produced. At the Moser site, twenty-six separate manufacturers are represented by marks that could be pinpointed to place of production. Their goods date throughout the occupation. Goods came from nine states in the United States, including the Midwest, the North, and the Northeast, and from England, Germany, and the Far East.

For example, many of the ceramics came from the Staffordshire potteries of England, a world center for ceramic production since the mid 1700s. Dishes also came from a center of U.S. production, around East Liverpool in Columbiana County, Ohio. Marked glass medicine bottles came from Pennsylvania, Missouri, Massachusetts, and Illinois. Marked glass canning jars and the white glass lid liners for the threaded zinc caps came from Pennsylvania, West Virginia, and New York. Such finds confirm that the Moser families, throughout the life of the farmstead, were dependent on distant factories and elaborate intermediate distribution systems for much that they used during their routine daily life.

The second means of estimating intensity of outside contact etically is by a search for tablewares such as dishes and glasswares that share patterns of decoration. The ability of factories to produce identically decorated pieces in great quantities represents a key element in understanding the results of mass production of consumer goods. Sets of dishes, glasses, or other table items could then be sold by merchants who could also provide replacement pieces in case of breakage. The consumer, of course, always has at least the possible option of avoiding the offering of sets and buying piecemeal. The choice of sets therefore implies familiarity with the desirability of symmetry in the kitchen cabinet and on the table. It also implies some acceptance of the values of conformity and subordination to the group that are reinforced by rigid uniformity of pattern, uniformity only slightly mediated by individual place settings within the rigid landscape of the table (see Deetz 1972, 1977 for the initial discussion of order and symmetry and their implications as revealed in industrially produced ceramics).

The rich deposit of trash at the Moser site indicated that sets were present and valued in the Moser family households throughout the occupation. For example, the trash in the root cellar under the kitchen ell of the house represented some 60 percent of the total artifacts recovered from the site. When the ceramic and glass tablewares from that cellar deposit were examined for set membership, nearly 25 percent of 118 vessels represented belonged to sets. Since at least two vessels from the same pattern must be recovered to confirm the presence of a set, additional sets might be represented by some of the patterns represented only by single artifacts.

At least six sets of ceramic dishes are represented at the site, including basic whitewares and the more expensive porcelains. There were also sets of stemmed glasses, tumblers, glass candy dishes, and glass bowls with matching lids. There are at least three sets of cutlery present, with bone handles, alloy fittings, and iron forks or knife blades.

The presence of tablewares in sets is a strong indication that the people acquiring those items were aware of the availability and desirability of matched tablewares. It also confirms that they were sharing symbols of fashion and prosperity with others far beyond Arkansas and the Ozarks. The Moser families did indeed belong to an information network extending beyond their immediate neighbors. And they reiterated that membership every time they sat down to eat.

That products made around the United States and the world should end up discarded at the Moser farmstead before 1919 does not mean that its inhabitants were cosmopolitan, nor does it mean that all the items came from so far away. It does suggest in a compelling way that the Moser inhabitants were integrated with world economic and information systems. This is quite a contrast to the motif of proud self-sufficiency symbolized in the Ozark Tradition Myth. The etic archeological data and the emic informant data suggest that the families at Moser had few such illusions.

WHAT ABOUT ISOLATION?

If independence is a major theme in the Ozark Tradition Myth, the very foundation of the myth rests on a presumption of isolation. According to the myth, isolation necessitated independence, and it also brought about familial incest, backwardness, ignorance, and self-reliance. Mythic isolation also permitted maintenance of medieval English folkways, including quaint Chaucerian speech patterns, quaint folksongs, and quaint folk beliefs. According to the myth, it was isolation that led somehow to the supposed uniqueness of the region's practices.

It is not the purpose of this paper to attempt a reexamination of the meaning and extent of isolation throughout the history of human occupation of the Ozarks, but all assertions of isolation must be taken with caution. For example, in spite of parallel assertions of isolation of prehistory populations in the Ozarks, recent archeological research on the prehistoric of the region indicates that the uplands did not offer impenetrable barriers in much of the last twelve thousand years (Sabo, Waddell, and House 1982; Brown 1984). The data from the Moser site clearly indicate ease of penetration after 1875 by dealers or agents selling everything from pump organs (one was in the living room of the house before World War I) to agricultural implements to fine European and Asian porcelain tablewares. The Yankee clock peddler is a staple of Ozark lore, but somehow he is forgotten whenever isolation is being praised or condemned.

Perhaps the single artifact that most reflects vistas wider than just an Ozark creek bottom was not intended for farm or table use. It was a souvenir of the Chicago World's Fair of 1893. This brass frame to a cloth badge, on which is stamped "Columbian Exposition Chicago 1893," may have been acquired by a member of the Sharp family, in-laws of Jeff and Rosy Moser, who lived at the farmstead from the 1880s to 1904. The Sharps had a reputation for progressiveness and prosperity, and Chicago was only a little more than a day's travel by train. The badge may have been given to the Sharps by a more widely travelled acquaintance. No matter how the badge reached the site, the recovery of a souvenir of an international celebration of technology and progress at a farmstead in a region at the time when the Ozark Tradition Myth was being created raises many questions about the accuracy of assertions of general isolation.

Some might claim that the Moser site is too easily accessible since it is not in the deepest recesses of the steepest mountains, but such a question begs the issue. Certainly the introduction and spread of railroads after 1875 in the rolling Springfield Plateau country of northwestern Arkansas and Missouri did offer commercial opportunities more easily exploited than where rails did not reach. Certainly one could be cut off from access to the industrial world for short periods during bad weather, or by intense poverty, or by a variety of other factors. However, to say that isolation was the norm throughout the Ozark uplands is to ignore a great deal of contrary data: the very economic underpinnings of the farm establishment depended on regional and material markets for the sale of livestock. The surviving physical evidence of glass canning jars, ceramic dishes, and cast iron cook pots visible in celebrated photographs of Ozark log cabin interiors (Godsey 1977) and in recent collections (McDonough 1975; Massey 1978) give the lie to isolation.

CONCLUSION

The Moser data have been used here to briefly examine certain aspects of the Ozark Tradition Myth. Other mythic themes are also present at the site but have not been treated. These include the outmigration of Arkansans to California, documented at Moser when John and Laura Sharp moved there for her health in 1904. Another theme, the disruptions, excitement, and potential for change introduced by World War I, appears when the Sharps' son Earl left the Moser farmstead in

1917 to go off to the Great War. And finally, the conflicting attractions of the known and the unknown are illustrated in the decisions that kept one brother, Dallas Moser, within a few miles of the family homeplace all his life while other brothers left never to return.

When research first began at the Moser site there was little knowledge of who lived there and when. The property itself was only known vaguely and by a few as "the old Sharp place." It is now known that the Moser farmstead was established in the 1870s at a time of intensive exploitation of the Ozark landscape by rowcropping. The Moser farmstead met its end with the end of rowcropping in the uplands and the consolidation of farms that came about with the transition to expanded pasturage for beef cattle. Not long after the end of the Great War what had once been a center of rural life had become merely another piece of pasture, a fate shared with hundreds of other farmsteads.

The Moser occupation makes a valuable addition to the Ozark story. In some ways the Moser information supports the often celebrated themes of independence, self-sufficiency, and pride in family accomplishment. In other ways, the Moser record forces one to think about other mythic themes, including isolation, backwardness, and insularity. Many of the contradictions in the Ozark Tradition Myth, at least for the late nineteenth century, can thus be seen as the result of the interaction between what people perceived as what they could do, what they should do, and what they had to do. When some of those actions are exaggerated and others ignored, when assumptions prevail instead of data, and when manufactured color is substituted for the complexities of human life, it becomes possible to deceive ourselves about where we have come and perhaps where we are going.

The irony of the Moser site data is that if the site had not been in the fabled Ozarks the presence of manufactured goods and the oral data about economic concerns with the wider world would have been of little surprise. It is the acceptance of the Ozark Tradition Myth, even by scholars, as an accurate representation of past reality that leads to shock at seeing fine ceramics, stemmed glassware, and a souvenir of a world's fair come out of the ground at what otherwise seems to be a traditional farmstead. It was the myth that led to misconceptions, not the daily routines of the people who lived ordinary and now forgotten lives.

REFERENCES

Brown, James A., 1984. *Prehistoric Southern Ozarks Marginality: A Myth Exposed*. Special Publication of the Missouri Archeological Society, No. 6 (Columbia, Mo.: Missouri Archeological Society).
Cochran, Robert, and Michael Luster, 1979. *For Love and Money: The Writings of Vance Randolph*. Arkansas College Folklore Archive Publications, Monograph No. 2 (Batesville, Ark.: Arkansas College Folklore Archives Publications).
Davis, Hester A., 1982. Operating Plans. In *A State Plan for the Conservation of Archeological Resources in Arkansas*, Hester A. Davis, ed. Arkansas Archeological Survey Research Series, No. 21 (Fayetteville, Ark.: Arkansas Archeological Survey), pp. OP1–OP54.
Deetz, James J. F., 1972. Ceramics from Plymouth, 1635–1835: The Archaeological Evidence. In *Ceramics in America*, Ian M. G. Quimby, ed. Winterhur Conference Report 1972 (Charlottesville, Va.: University Press of Virginia), pp. 15–40.
_____, 1977. *In Small Things Forgotten: The Archeology of Early American Life* (Garden City, N.Y.: Anchor Press/Doubleday).
Godsey, Townsend, 1977. *Ozarks Mountain Folk: These Were the Last* (Branson, Mo.: The Ozarks Mountaineer).
Harington, Donald, 1975. *The Architecture of the Arkansas Ozarks* (New York: Little, Brown and Co.).
King, T. F., P. P. Hickman, and C. Berg, 1977. *Anthropology in Historic Preservation: Caring for Culture's Clutter* (New York: Academic Press).
Massey, Ellen Gray, 1978. *Bittersweet Country* (New York: Anchor Press/Doubleday).
McDonough, Nancy, 1975. *Garden Sass: A Catalog of Arkansas Folkways* (New York: Coward McCann and Gehegan).
Page, Tate C., 1977. *The Voices of Moccasin Creek* (Point Lookout, Mo.: School of the Ozarks Press).
Price, James F., and Cynthia R. Price, 1978. *An Investigation of Settlement Patterns and Subsistence on the Ozark Escarpment in Southeast Missouri during the First Half of the Nineteenth Century* (Columbia, Mo.: American Archeology Division, University of Missouri).
Rafferty, Milton., 1980. *The Ozarks, Land and Life* (Norman: University of Oklahoma Press).
Rayburn, Otto E., 1941. *Ozark Country* (New York: Duell Sloan and Pearce).
Sabo, George III, David B. Waddell, and John H. House, 1982. *A Cultural Resource Overview of the Ozark--St. Francis National Forests, Arkansas*

(Russellville, Ark.: U.S. Department of Agriculture, Forest Service, Southern Region).

Santeford, Lawrence Gene, William A. Martin, and E. Thomas Hemmings, 1985. *Excavation at Four Sites in the Cypress Creek Basin.* Arkansas Archeological Survey Research Report, No. 24 (Fayetteville, Ark.: Arkansas Archeological Survey).

Schuyler, Robert L., ed., 1978. *Historical Archaeology: A Guide to Substantive and Theoretical Contributions* (Greenwood, N.J.: Baywood Publishing Co.).

Stewart-Abernathy, Leslie C., 1985. *Independent but not Isolated: The Archeology of a Late Nineteenth Century Ozark Farmstead.* Arkansas Archeological Survey Research Series, in press (Fayetteville, Ark.: Arkansas Archeological Survey).

Stewart-Abernathy, Leslie C., and Beverly S. Watkins, 1982. Historical Archeology. In *A State Plan for the Conservation of Archeological Resources in Arkansas.* Arkansas Archeological Survey Research Series, No. 21 (Fayetteville, Ark.: Arkansas Archeological Survey), pp. HA1–HA97.

Wolf, John Quincy, 1974. *Life in the Leatherwoods* (Memphis: Memphis State University Press).

Frontier Settlement in the Current River Valley: Variation in Organizational Patterning

Cynthia R. Price

The eastern Ozark Highland of southeast Missouri and northeast Arkansas was settled during the early part of the nineteenth century by groups from the old Upland South.[1] During the frontier period, settlement throughout the region generally fit the organizational pattern characteristic of the immigrant Upland South culture as defined by geographers, historians, and anthropologists (for example, Newton 1974; Arensberg 1955; Arensberg and Kimball 1965). Despite the general similarity of settlement from a regional perspective, differences in the organizational and community structures are evident on a local level. These local variations reflect differences in cultural adaptation which are lost in the broad pattern but which are necessary for understanding the variety of frontier responses.

Local variations in organization are evident in the frontier settlement along the Current River. Although the upper and lower parts of the valley were settled at about the same time by people with similar ethnic backgrounds (primarily Scotch-Irish; Clendenen 1973; Flanders 1979), different settlement patterns, reflecting different organizational structures, characterize the two parts of the valley. To understand these differences, a more detailed study was made of one aspect of the sociocultural system, economic development, which is one of the variables influencing the organizational structure of a population and the resultant settlement patterns. The following study uses both historical/documentary and archeological data to examine the settlement systems and the relationship between these systems and economic development in the upper and lower Current River Valley.

THE STUDY AREA

The Current River is one of the principal streams draining the eastern Ozarks in southeast Missouri (Figure 1). Initially, the entire valley area was part of Lawrence County, Arkansas/Missouri, which took in nearly all of southern Missouri and northern Arkansas. Following Missouri statehood in 1820, the southern half of Missouri belonged to Wayne County. In 1833, Ripley County was formed and included nearly the entire Current River Valley. In 1840, Shannon County, lying along the upper Current and its principal tributary, the Jacks Fork, was separated from Ripley County, and in 1859, Carter County, lying just below Shannon along the middle stretch of the river, was formed. The following study focuses on the areas now included in Shannon, Carter, and Ripley counties (Figure 1) from the time of earliest settlement until the 1860s when the Civil War disrupted the economy and settlement of the area (see Flanders 1979). Shannon County represents the upper Current River Valley, and Ripley and Carter counties represent the middle and lower valley, respectively.

SETTLEMENT AND ORGANIZATION PATTERNS

Societies or cultural groups may organize their activities in a variety of ways, the organization reflecting the integrating mechanisms operant in the group or cultural system. The organization is reflected in the settlement system with its observable patterns on the landscape. The level of organization considered in this study is that of the community. As noted by Lewis (1976:88), community is defined functionally and should be seen in an organizational rather than a spatial sense. Geographical boundaries may, however, be imposed. A community is composed of functionally distinct settlements, patterned on the landscape and reflecting the sociocultural organizational mechanisms of a population. The settlements form a hierarchy of settlement types, each of which serves a particular function in the political, social, and economic systems of the community. The kinds, number, and locations of the various settlements in a community are dependent on the organizational requirements of the populations. Community form is not static. Settlement function may change through time as the frontier matures or

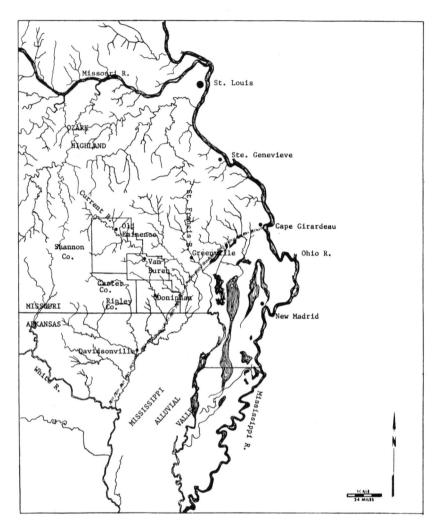

Figure 1
The Location of the Study Area in Southeast Missouri.

changes, and community form may change as the adaptive responses of the population change (Lewis 1976:88).

The community form recognized in the eastern Ozarks during the frontier period corresponds most closely to the "open country neighborhood" or "crossroads hamlet" as described by Arensberg and Kimball (1965:108–112), in which dispersed settlement units are loosely organized into townships and/or counties. In this region, the community generally corresponds to the county, and the county was the broadest unit of organization below the state level. Newton (1974:150) notes that "only in the county unit can one find all aspects of Upland-South society."

Generally, the settlement hierarchy of the eastern Ozarks counties included one county seat settlement, one or more hamlets, and scattered domestic habitations (such as farmsteads or hunter cabins) and specialized activity loci. The county seat town, which corresponds to the frontier town in the functional models of Lewis (1984:22–23), was central to the county organization. These settlements served to centralize social, political, and economic activities. They are usually the largest settlements in the county or community and are expected to manifest their centralizing function in the number and range of structures present. The majority of structures should reflect the performance of activities such as small scale manufacturing and maintenance; transfer and storage of goods and commodities; and political and social activities associated with the periodic gatherings of persons for collective purposes such as trials, markets, and tavern socializing. Below the courthouse town in the settlement hierarchy are nucleated settlements or small hamlets. These were not formally platted but were simply an aggregation of settlements usually around a mill and/or store (Newton 1974:151). Specialized activity centers such as mills, secondary trading establishments, extractive and manufacturing loci, and individual households such as cabins or farmsteads were dispersed throughout the countryside.

The settlement hierarchies in the counties lying along the Current River valley are similar to that described above, with one exception. The counties on the lower and middle Current River (early Lawrence and later Ripley and Carter counties) had county seat towns serving centralizing functions, but Shannon County on the upper Current is distinctly different. It lacked a formal county seat town for the first thirty years of its existence, and the centralizing functions usually ascribed to the county seat were each to be found in separate settlements. The functions of these early county seat settlements can be assessed using both documentary and archeological data. In the lower Current, these settlements included Davidsonville (ca. 1815–1830), the county seat of Lawrence County (Smith 1973; Dollar 1977; Stewart-Abernathy 1980); Old Greenville (ca. 1818–1940) in Wayne County (Price and Price 1979); Doniphan (ca. 1840–present) in Ripley County (Federal Census, Population Schedules, Ripley County 1850–1860); and Old Van Buren (ca. 1834–1860), the first county seat of Ripley County and later of Carter County (Ripley County Deed Records Book A:12–16; U.S. War Department I[13]:230–231; Oakley 1970:34). All of these towns were platted with a central courthouse square. In addition to the courthouse and jail, Davidsonville, Doniphan, and Old Greenville included at least one trading establishment, an inn or tavern, and several residences, and there was a mill at Doniphan and Old Greenville. Old Van Buren contained at least several residences and a mill. The settlement at Davidsonville occupied forty-two acres and that at Old Greenville twenty-one acres (settlement size is not available for the other settlements). All of the towns were on broad river terraces with room for expansion. The important thing about the towns for the purposes of this study is their presence in a formal sense.

Documentary and especially archeological information for Old Eminence, the county seat of Shannon County from its formation in 1840 until the Civil War, presents a very different picture. There is no evidence that the town was ever formally platted. There were only two structures present, a courthouse and a jail, and there was never anyone in residence (Federal Census, Population Schedules, Shannon County 1860; Elliott 1902:34; Price 1984). The archeological data suggest that the range of activities at Old Eminence was narrow and the structures did not serve multiple functions (Price 1984). Old Eminence occupied less than one acre and was located on a small terrace remnant with little room for expansion. The settlement may best be called an isolated political center (Lewis 1976:230). Economic activities were centered in a store located several miles below Old Eminence (Price 1981b; Deatherage Store Account Book). It was not until after the Civil War that a formally platted town was established as the county seat some twenty miles from the old settlement. In the upper valley, then, political and economic activities were certainly centered in separate dispersed settlements, each serving only one principal function. In the middle and lower valley these activities were centered in one place, at least formally.

COUNTY ECONOMICS

The differences in the two forms of settlement in the upper and lower Current River Valley can in part be explained by the differences in economic development and organizational requirements in the two areas. Settlers with different subsistence requirements occupied the entire valley from the time of early settlement on (Price, Price, and Harris 1976:142–150; Price and Price 1981; Price 1981c; see also Babcock 1965; Bek 1929; Bell 1957; Featherstonhaugh 1968; Gerstaeker 1965; James 1972; Schoolcraft 1821, 1853). Hunter-herders were highly mobile and relied primarily on hunting, trapping, and trading, with little emphasis on agriculture. Agriculturalists relied on domestic production and hunting-herding to varying degrees. At the lower end of the agricultural scale the settlers cultivated small plots of land, maintained small herds of livestock, and hunted and trapped for subsistence and trade. At the upper end of the scale were individuals who may parallel the planter of the Old South in the exploitation of slave labor and participation in a nonlocal market economy (Mooney 1957; Mintz 1959; Denman 1978). Individuals engaged in commercial sawmilling were also in residence. The configuration of the various groups locally and their social, political, and economic needs influence the organizational structure of the community or county. Although settlers from both ends of the subsistence scale (from hunter-herders to farmers and manufacturers) were present in both the upper and lower Current River Valley, the combination of groups was different and economic development proceeded along different lines in the two areas. This can be seen in the differences in agricultural development, development of manufacturing, and in the homogeneity or heterogeneity of the population.

Agricultural Development

Agriculturalists, including small-scale farmers as well as those who might be called planters, were present in all parts of the valley from at least as early as the second decade of the nineteenth century (Price

Table 1
Farm Size in Ripley, Carter, and Shannon Counties, 1850 and 1860

Number of Improved Acres	Number of Farms				
	1850		1860		
	Shannon	Ripley/Carter	Shannon	Carter	Ripley
0	2	4	4	0	0
1–10	25	35	126	13	12
11–20	69	103	141	34	52
21–30	32	51	67	28	55
31–40	16	50	33	21	48
41–50	6	25	9	6	33
51–60	4	5	6	7	19
61–70	4	11	3	5	11
71–80	0	3	5	4	11
81–90	1	2	1	3	2
91–100	0	3	4	5	5
101–150	0	0	2	1	6
151–200	0	0	1	1	3
200+	0	1	0	0	1
TOTALS	157	293	402	128	258

1981a, 1983, 1984; Orchard and Orchard 1977) and along with the manufacturers came to dominate county economics. By 1850, at least 85 percent of the population in all parts of the valley reported farming as their occupation (Federal Census, Population Schedules, Shannon and Ripley counties 1850). Although settlement increased in all parts of the valley during the first half of the nineteenth century, agricultural development in Shannon County on the upper Current remained almost static while that of Ripley and Carter counties on the middle and lower Current expanded. Differences in development can be seen in the information in the Agricultural Schedules, Federal Census, for Shannon, Ripley, and Carter counties for the years 1850 and 1860 (Tables 1, 2, 3). The differences in the two areas are most evident in average farm size, as measured by number of improved acres, and in grain production. In 1850, the average farm size in number of improved acres was similar in both areas, twenty-three acres in Shannon County and

Table 2
Farm and Population Information, Ripley, Carter, and Shannon
Counties, 1850 and 1860

	1850		1860		
	Shannon	Ripley	Shannon	Carter	Ripley
Total farms	157	293	402	128	258
Total acres cultivated	3,613	8,310	9,841	4,603	10,930
Average farm size[a]	23	28	24	36	42
% farms less than 40 acres	90	81	91	75	60
% farms less than 30 acres	80	64	83	59	46
% farms more than 70 acres	1	3	3	11	11
Population	1,104	2,814	2,271	4,769[b]	

[a]Size is measured in improved acres in this table.
[b]Population of Carter and Ripley counties combined.

twenty-eight acres in Ripley County (including Carter County, which was constituted in 1859) (Tables 1 and 2). By 1860 both the number of farms and the total number of acres under cultivation had increased in all three counties. The average farm size in Shannon County, however, remained nearly constant at twenty-four acres but increased in the middle and lower Current to thirty-six acres in Carter County and forty-two acres in Ripley County. The percentage of farms below thirty and forty acres in size changed little from 1850 to 1860 in Shannon County, but in Ripley and Carter counties the percentage was greatly reduced and by 1860 was nearly one-half the percentage for Shannon County (46 percent in Ripley County and 91 percent in Shannon County). From 1850 to 1860, the population of Shannon County increased by 205 percent, the number of farms increased by 256 percent, and the total number of acres under cultivation increased by 272 percent. In Ripley/ Carter County, the population increase from 1850 to 1860 was only 169 percent, the number of farms increased by 132 percent, and the acres under cultivation increased 187 percent. The pattern in the upper Current Valley, then, was an increase in the number of small farms through time; in the lower part of the valley there was a smaller actual increase in the number of farms but an expansion of production on a greater number of farms.

Table 3
Farm Production, Ripley, Carter, and Shannon Counties,
1850 and 1860

	1850		1860		
	Shannon	Ripley	Shannon	Carter	Ripley
Farms reporting	156	288	309	115	242
Horses	519	1,047	709	407	937
Average per farm	3	3	2	3	4
Farms reporting	149	278	302	115	249
Swine	4,569	10,397	5,599	2,726	5,674
Average per farm	30	37	18	24	23
Farms reporting	137	248	328	117	245
Cattle	771	1,899	1,977	591	2,481
Average per farm	5	7	6	5	10
Farms reporting	104	171	229	83	167
Sheep	1,367	1,496	2,904	1,015	2,410
Average per farm	13	8	12	12	14
Farms reporting	155	267	391	127	257
Bushels of corn	56,713	113,241	145,140	98,176	127,480
Average per farm	365	424	371	773	496

Along with the increase in average farm size in the lower Current from 1850 to 1860, the census records indicate that there was an increase in production of grains as measured in average number of bushels of corn per farm (Table 3). Livestock production, however, remained relatively constant in both parts of the valley (Table 3). The increase in farm size and average corn production per farm in the lower counties suggests that there was a greater emphasis on commercial agriculture in that area. Indeed, there was a commercial pork slaughterhouse in operation in Ripley County in 1850 (Federal Census, Products of Industry, Ripley County 1850).

The differences in agricultural development in the two parts of the valley are in part attributable to local topography and transportation networks. Shannon County, on the extreme upper Current, is characterized by more rugged terrain than the counties lying along the Ozark Escarpment downstream. Interfluves are steeper and the streams swifter and shallower. The configuration of trade and transportation networks, both local and nonlocal, was different in the two areas. The lower Current is crossed by one and probably two major overland travel routes. The Natchitoches Trace, present from prehistoric times to the twentieth century, ran from St. Louis to Texas following the rolling foothills of the escarpment. It crossed the Current near the Missouri/Arkansas line. Another possible major road crossed the river in Carter County just below Van Buren. No such regional or panregional roads have been identified in the upper Current to date. In the upper Current the steep interfluves make overland travel difficult. Although local travel is more often by water than by land in the upper Current, the Current River is more easily navigated in the middle and lower reaches than in the upper, where it tends to be seasonally shallow and swift. The opportunities for agricultural expansion during the years of initial settlement, then, were more limited in the upper Current. Although the Shannon County population increased at a greater rate than that of Ripley County and the number of farms continued to increase rapidly, size and productive capability as well as market access were held in check by the physical characteristics of the land. The settlers in the lower Current had greater access to wide-reaching trade routes present at the time of earliest settlement.

Manufacturing

Resource exploitative industries and manufacturing also developed to a greater extent in Ripley and Carter counties. The principal industry was pine lumber production. During the 1830s, and possibly earlier, at least one or two mills were in operation in Shannon County (Ripley County Deed Records Book A:36; Orchard and Orchard 1977:88; Price 1983), and at least three were operating in the lower Current (Pitman 1834; Price 1985; L. A. Snider and Company). By 1860, there were at least six or seven separate milling operations in Carter and Ripley counties but only two were reported in Shannon County (Federal Census, Products of Industry and Population Schedules, Ripley, Carter, and Shannon counties 1860). The lumber products were not only used locally but were exported, usually by rafting downstream (Pitman 1834; Sauer 1920; Orchard and Orchard 1977:88; L. A. Snider and Company). Although pine timber was as plentiful in the upper Current as in the lower, the swiftness and seasonal shallowness of the streams made the rafting of lumber products more difficult there than in the middle and lower Current.

Population Composition

The relative degree of sociocultural heterogeneity or homogeneity of a population is also a measure of the organizational complexity of the group. The degree of differentiation in the population can be seen in the relative degrees of specialization in occupations in the two areas. In 1850, 95 percent of the people in Shannon County listed farming or farm laborer as their occupation; 89 percent did so in Ripley County. Only eight occupations other than farming are listed for Shannon County; twenty-four different occupations are listed for Ripley County (Tables 4 and 5). The occupations listed for Shannon County in 1850 were those involving repair or maintenance and production of items which could have been used locally. Only one service occupation, minister, is listed. In Ripley County, a number of service occupations are reported, such as teacher, physician, and lawyer, as well as retail merchants, commercial manufacturers (sawmillers and lumber dealers), and local manufacturing and repair such as smithing, shoemaker, and seamstress. In 1860, Shannon County reported ten different occupations apart from agriculture which included a few more service occupations along with several retailers. Ripley County reported twenty-four, and Carter County eighteen (twenty-six different occupations for Carter and Ripley counties combined). The town of Doniphan alone reported ten different occupations that year.

The number of black and mulatto slaves in the population of the three counties was also significantly different. In 1850, the total number of slaves in Shannon County was nine and in Ripley County eighty-five. In 1860, there were thirteen slaves in Shannon County, seventy-eight in Ripley County, and eighteen in Carter County (Federal Census, Population and Slave Schedules, Ripley, Carter, and Shannon counties 1850, 1860). The slaves were used in the household, in farming, and in sawmilling.

INTERPRETATIONS AND CONCLUSIONS

Although all of the settlers, from the hunter-herders to the manufacturers, were of necessity tied into the economic system, those at the upper end of the continuum engaged in manufacture and commercial agriculture were perhaps more closely tied to county economics. Successful competition and marketing of commercial products require a greater and/or more formal organizational network. A greater number of commercial enterprises may also increase the need for centralized political organization. The county court system and the state government, through the county organization, were both involved in expanding and improving trade networks as well as in regulating local retailing of goods and services. The county court had jurisdiction over local road improvements and the state government over state roads and navigable waterways, including the Current River, which was the principal route of shipment of pine lumber and possibly of agricultural products as well (Laws of Missouri 1840:234, 1843:393, 1854:181–183; Pitman 1834; Ripley County Records 1834–1860; Lawrence County Records 1815–1834). Therefore, the organization in the middle and lower Current, where the larger farms and greater number of milling enterprises were concentrated, would be expected to be more centralized. The greater number of establishments engaged in commercial enterprises undoubtedly produced a greater number of wealthy or upper-class citizens in Carter and Ripley counties. This group in turn would support a wider variety of service occupations, increasing local organizational complexity. The small family farmers and hunter-herders would have need for trading establishments only to market products or trade for the purchase of goods for household use. Lesser wealth left less room for support of a service class.

The net result was a rapid proliferation of small farms with a less differentiated population in the upper Current, a less centralized organization, and a settlement system without a single central town to serve a variety of functions. Topographic and transportation constraints limited commercial expansion. In the lower Current commercial production expanded until the Civil War. Organizational complexity and greater population differentiation went hand in hand.

The differences in the settlement of the valley may also be seen as the differences in a core settlement area and the hinterland. Although organized into individual counties, the various parts of the river were also tied together in a regional settlement network. The lower Current was the original core area; the upper valley its hinterland. During the time of earliest settlement the two parts of the valley were parts of the same county or community organization, but the county seat town,

Table 4
Reported Occupations, Shannon and Ripley
Counties, 1850

Shannon		Ripley	
Occupation	No.	Occupation	No.
Farmer	240	Farmer	584
Laborer	24	Laborer	45
Blacksmith	3	Blacksmith	13
Carpenter	3	Carpenter	8
Wagonmaker	1	Laborer	1
Miller	2	Miller	3
Cooper	1	Laborer	1
Minister	1	Millwright	2
Slater	1	Laborer	1
Collier	1	Cooper	1
		Lumbermaker	6
		Laborer	6
		Lumber dealer	1
		Sawyer	1
		Ox-driver	1
		Tailor	1
		Wagonmaker	1
		Stonemason	1
		Grocer	1
		Laborer	1
		Shoemaker	3
		Physician	2
		Laborer	1
		Turner	3
		Merchant	5
		Lawyer	1
		Schoolteacher	4
		Mail carrier	1
		Clerk of court	1
		Student	1
		Sadler	1
		Tanner	4

Table 5
Reported Occupations, Shannon, Carter, and Ripley Counties, 1860

Shannon		Carter		Ripley	
Occupation	No.	Occupation	No.	Occupation	No.
Farmer	396	Farmer	240	Farmer	652
Laborer	168	Laborer	31	Laborer	142
Wheelwright	1	Minister	2	Wheelwright	1
Wagonmaker	1	Painter	1	Seamstress	6[a]
Millwright	1	Bootmaker	1	Tailor	1
Carpenter	1	Carpenter	4	Physician	5[a]
Civil engineer	1	Wagonmaker	2	Carpenter	6
Physician	4	Shoemaker	1	Merchant	7[a]
Seamstress	4	Physician	2	Miller	1
Merchant	2	Gunsmith	1	House carpenter	6[a]
Minister	1	Collier	1	Smith	12[a]
Schoolteacher	1	Clerk of court	2	Millwright	1
		Schoolteacher	3	Wool carder	1
		Millwright	1	Mechanic	3
		Blacksmith	4	Moulder	1
		Cigarmaker	1	Painter	1
		Merchant	1	Schoolteacher	2
		Basketmaker	1	Minister	2
		Surveyor	2	Sheriff	1
				Tinner	3
				Midwife	1
				Dramshop keeper	1[a]
				Well digger	1[a]
				Lawyer	1[a]
				Clerk	1[a]
				Washer	1[a]

[a] At least one listed in the town of Doniphan.

Davidsonville, was much nearer the lower Current. Only during the second and third generation of settlement was the early county subdivided and the county system repeated along the river. The hinterland originally, the upper Current only lately came to resemble the original core in its organizational structure. Finally, this study underscores the flexibility and adaptability of the Upland South organizational pattern brought in with the earliest immigrants (Newton 1974) and modified and stabilized to meet the changing environmental and sociocultural conditions.

NOTE

1. Funding for the archeological work in the Current River valley, including survey and the excavations at Old Eminence, and for a part of the study of the documentary records used here was provided by the National Park Service, Midwest Archeological Center, Lincoln, Nebraska. Part of the funding for the excavations at Old Eminence and Isaac Kelley Plantation was also provided by the University of Nebraska through its summer Field School in Archeology.

REFERENCES

Arensberg, Conrad M., 1955. American Communities. *American Anthropologist* 57: 1143–1162.

Arensberg, Conrad M., and Solon T. Kimball, 1965. *Culture and Community* (New York: Harcourt, Brace and World).

Babcock, Rufus, ed., 1965. *Forty Years of Pioneer Life: Memoir of John Mason Peck, D.D., Edited from His Journal and Correspondence* (reprint of the 1864 edition; Carbondale: Southern Illinois University Press).

Bek, William G., trans. and ed., 1929. George Engelmann, Man of Science. Parts I–III. *Missouri Historical Review* 23(2):197–206, 23(3):427–446, 23(4):517–535.

Bell, John R., 1957. The Journal of Captain John R. Bell, Official Journalist for the Stephen H. Long Expedition to the Rocky Mountains, 1820. In *The Far West and the Rockies Historical Series 1820–1875*. Vol. 6, Harlan M. Fuller and Leroy R. Hafner, eds. (Glendale, Calif.: Arthur Clark Co.).

Clendenen, H., 1973. Settlement Morphology of the Southern Courtois Hills, Missouri, 1820–1860. Ph.D. dissertation, Louisiana State University.

Deatherage Store Account Book, 1856. *Account Book* (St. Louis: The Missouri Historical Society).

Denman, Davis, 1978. Agriculture, Diet, and Economic Status: Subsistence Strategies 1850–1870, Ripley County, Missouri, with Particularistic Analysis of the Widow Harris Cabin Site (manuscript on file with the Southwest Missouri State University, Center for Archaeological Research, Southeast Field Station, Naylor).

Dollar, Clyde, 1977. *An Archaeological Assessment of Historic Davidsonville, Arkansas*. Arkansas Archeological Survey, Research Report, No. 17. (Fayetteville, Ark.: Arkansas Archeological Survey).

Elliott, General Isaac H., 1902. *History of the Thirty-third Regiment Illinois Veteran Volunteer Infantry in the Civil War, 22nd August, 1861 to 7th December, 1865* (Gibson City, Ill.).

Featherstonhaugh, George William, 1968. *Excursion through the Slave States* (reprint of the 1844 edition; New York: Negro Universities Press).

Federal Census Records. *Population, Agriculture, Slave, and Industry Schedules.* Wayne County, Missouri, 1830; Ripley County, Missouri, 1840, 1850, 1860; Carter County, Missouri, 1860; Shannon County, Missouri, 1850, 1860 (copies on file with the Center for Archaeological Research, Southeast Field Station, Southwest Missouri State University, Naylor).

Flanders, Robert, 1979. Regional History. In *Cultural Resource Overview in the Mark Twain National Forest,* Mary L. Douthit, ed. Center for Archaeological Research Report, No. 94 (Springfield: Southwest Missouri State University), pp. 114–282.

Gerstaeker, Friedrich, 1965. *Wild Sports in the Far West* (reprint of the 1854 English translation; Durham, N.C.: Duke University Press).

James, Edwin, 1972. *Account of an Expedition from Pittsburg to the Rocky Mountains Performed in the Years 1819, 1820* (reprint of the 1823 edition; Mass.: Imprint Society).

L. A. Snider and Company, *1832–1870: Account Books of L. A. Snider and Company, Pike Creek, Missouri* (Columbia, Mo.: F. B. Green Collection, Joint Manuscripts Collection, State Historical Society).

Lawrence County Records. *Records, Lawrence County, Arkansas* (Lawrence County Courthouse, Walnut Ridge, Ark.).

Laws of Missouri, 1840. *Laws of the State of Missouri Passed at the First Session of the Eleventh General Assembly.*

———, 1843. *Laws of the State of Missouri Passed at the Session of the Twelfth General Assembly.*

———, 1854. *Laws of the State of Missouri Passed at the Session of the Eighteenth General Assembly.*

Lewis, Kenneth E., 1976. *Camden, a Frontier Town in Eighteenth Century*

South Carolina. Anthropological Studies 2. Institute of Archaeology and Anthropology (Columbia: University of South Carolina).

_____, 1984. The American Frontier, an Archaeological Study of Settlement Pattern and Process (New York: Academic Press).

Mintz, Sidney W., 1959. The Plantation as a Socio-cultural Type. In Plantation Systems of the New World. Pan-American Union, Social Science Monographs 7.

Mooney, Chase C., 1957. Slavery in Tennessee. Indiana University Publications, Social Science Series, No. 17 (Bloomington: Indiana University Press).

Newton, Milton, 1974. Cultural Preadaptation and the Upland South. In Man and Cultural Heritage: Papers in Honor of Fred B. Kniffer, H. J. Walker and W. B. Haag, eds., Geoscience and Man, vol. 5. (Baton Rouge: School of Geoscience, Louisiana State University), pp. 143–154.

Oakley, Gene, 1970. The History of Carter County (Van Buren, Mo.: J-G Publications).

Orchard, Charles L., and Marjory Orchard, 1977. The Chiltons, Their Ancestors and Descendants, vols. I and II. (Eminence, Mo.).

Pitman, Peyton, 1834. Letter from Peyton Pitman, Current River, Missouri, to D. K. Pitman, February 2, 1834 (The Cape Girardeau County Historical Society, Jackson Public Library, Jackson, Mo.).

Price, Cynthia R., 1981a. Report of Initial Investigations at the Isaac Kelley Site, 23CT-111, in the Ozark National Scenic Riverways, Carter County, Missouri: 1980–1981. Report to the National Park Service–Midwest Archeological Center, Lincoln (Springfield: Southwest Missouri State University).

_____, 1981b. Old Eminence: Report of Initial Investigations in the Ozark National Scenic Riverways at the First County Seat of Shannon County, Missouri: 1980. Report to the National Park Service–Midwest Archeological Center, Lincoln (Springfield: Southwest Missouri State University).

_____, 1981c. Analysis of the Historic Period Materials and Assessment of Site Function. In Changing Settlement Systems in the Fourche Creek Watershed in the Ozark Border Region of Southeast Missouri and Northeast Arkansas, James E. Price and Cynthia R. Price, eds. Report to the Interagency Archaeological Services, Denver (Springfield: Southwest Missouri State University), pp. 625–676.

_____, 1983. Historical Archaeological Research: Literature Review. In Archaeological Investigations in the Ozark National Scenic Riverways, 1981–1982, by James E. Price, Cynthia R. Price, Roger Saucier, and Timothy Perttula. Report to the National Park Service–Midwest Archeological Center, Lincoln (Springfield: Southwest Missouri State University), pp. 25–191.

———, 1984. Excavations at the Historic Period Sites. In *Archaeological Investigations in the Ozark National Scenic Riverways, 1982–1983*, by James E. Price, Cynthia R. Price, Roger Saucier, Paul Delcourt, Hazel Delcourt, and Newman Smith. Report to the National Park Service–Midwest Archeological Center, Lincoln (Springfield: Southwest Missouri State University), pp. 14–165.

———, 1985. Excavations at the Historic Period Sites. In *Archaeological Investigations in the Ozark National Scenic Riverways, 1983–1984*. Report to the National Park Service–Midwest Archeological Center, Lincoln (Springfield: Southwest Missouri State University), pp. 13–142.

Price, Cynthia R., and James E. Price, 1981. Investigations of Settlement and Subsistence Systems in the Ozark Border Region of Southeast Missouri during the First Half of the 19th Century: The Widow Harris Cabin Project. *Ethnohistory* 28(3):237–258.

Price, James, Cynthia R. Price, and Suzanne E. Harris, 1976. *An Assessment of the Fourche Creek Watershed*. Report to the USDA–Soil Conservation Service (Columbia: University of Missouri).

Ripley County Records. *Records of Ripley County, Missouri* (Doniphan, Mo.: Ripley County Courthouse).

Sauer, Carl O., 1920. *The Geography of the Ozark Highland of Missouri* (Chicago: University of Chicago Press).

Schoolcraft, Henry R., 1821. *Journal of a Tour into the Interior of Missouri and Arkansas* (London: Sir Richard Phillips and Co.).

———, 1853. *Scenes and Adventures in the Semi-Alpine Region of the Ozark Mountains of Missouri and Arkansas* (Philadelphia: Lippincott, and Grambo and Company).

Smith, Samuel D., 1973. Prospectus for Historic Site Archaeology in Northeast Arkansas. *Craighead County Historical Quarterly* 11(2):7–17.

Stewart-Abernathy, Leslie C., 1980. *The Seat of Justice: 1815–1830, an Archaeological Reconnaissance of Davidsonville, 1979*. Arkansas Archeological Survey Research Report, No. 21 (Fayetteville, Ark.: Arkansas Archeological Survey).

U. S. War Department, 1880–1902. *The War of the Rebellion: A Compilation of the Official Records of the Union and Confederate Armies*. 70 vols., 128 books (Washington, D.C.: Government Printing Office).

Camp Meeting and Archaism in Southwestern Arkansas

James A. Rees, Jr.

Though it is actually named for the man who donated the land for the first encampment in 1884, I shall call it Bethel Methodist Camp Meeting. I do this to protect the identity and privacy of the camp meeting people, but I think they would approve of my choice of pseudonyms. Bethel means "house of God" and in the Old Testament it is the name given by Jacob to the holy place where he saw a vision of a ladder to heaven with angels ascending and descending (Genesis 28:12–19). No one there has ever reported a vision quite so dramatic as Jacob's, but for many sinners over the years the Bethel Camp Meeting has been something of a ladder to heaven. For this and other important reasons it is regarded by them as no less sacred a place.

It would be obvious in fact to anyone that Bethel campground is unique just by its appearance. It is located on the Gulf Coastal Plain of rural southwest Arkansas, a region once checkered by many small farms but now mostly given over to timber production and small cattle operations. Against this backdrop the campground presents a rather surprising landscape.

Bethel is situated in the bottomlands on the banks of Black Earth Creek. Parts of the grounds are always soggy and damp even in the driest August, and floods have occasionally broken up meetings in the past. It is certainly not a place one would choose to live year-round, but at camp meeting time in the late summer dog days it is cooled by the shade of towering water oaks, white oaks, and tupelo trees.

Under this green canopy is a remarkable collection of vernacular architecture which unenlightened outsiders might callously refer to as shacks but which the Bethel campers call "tents." Most of these tents stand side by side in a long horseshoe-shaped row facing inward toward the great open plaza which they form. In the center of the plaza is a large open-sided building with a tall, vented, hipped roof. Not far away, large concrete steps lead down to a pavement in the bottom of a ravine which forms the eastern boundary of the plaza. In the center of this pavement is an open concrete box in which a spring of cold blue water wells up and drains away into a small stream.

Together all of these elements—the shaded grove, the tents, the shed, the ever-flowing spring—were once familiar to millions in nineteenth-century America as the ideal setting for a camp meeting. Camp meetings sprang to life on the Kentucky frontier shortly after 1800. They were the most visible expression of a religious revival then sweeping the country and now known to historians as the "Second Great Awakening" (McLoughlin 1978) or simply the "Great Revival" (Boles 1972). The history of these early camp meetings is vividly examined in books by Charles Johnson (1955), John Boles (1972), and Dickson Bruce (1974). Bruce gives this description of them: "Camp meetings were annual gatherings at which people camped out for several days of preaching, praying, singing and above all, 'converting souls to the way.' Crowds often numbered in the thousands and came to the campsite from as far as fifty miles away. The camp meeting was by all accounts a significant frontier practice" (1974:51).

Started by Presbyterian ministers, the camp meetings were later taken over almost exclusively by the Methodists. Camp meetings soon appeared wherever there were Methodists. They had crossed the Ohio by 1803 and spread as far as New England, Canada, and California by the 1830s and 1840s. By 1840, camp meeting activity was on the decline. However, in the late nineteenth century a new wave of revivalism swept the country and camp meetings once again became popular. In this period they became a vehicle for the Holiness Movement which emerged among Methodists in the North just prior to the Civil War (Dieter 1980; Jones 1974).

In parts of the rural South, especially in Arkansas, there seems to have been renewed interest in old-style Methodist camp meetings in the late 1800s. These meetings had few if any Holiness elements, and like the first camp meetings were exclusively evangelistic in nature. Between 1870 and 1900 seven Methodist camp meetings were started in southern Arkansas (Baugh 1954). Bethel, which began in 1884, was one of these and is today the largest of only four remaining Methodist camp meetings in south Arkansas.

Although the sign at the entrance proclaims Bethel to be a Methodist camp meeting, its ties to the United Methodist Church are unofficial. Camp pastors have by tradition always been Methodists, but approximately 25 percent of the campers are not Methodists. There are Baptists, Presbyterians, and members of several other denominations who camp there. Everyone is careful not to offend anyone's denominational sensibilities. Under the shed the Methodist pastors adhere to a basic form of Southern Evangelical Protestantism similar to that described by Samuel Hill (1966:20–29) as being common to the major Protestant denominations in the South.

THE CAMP MEETING PEOPLE

The Bethel campers are a difficult group to define. They exhibit few traits, other than their common participation in the camp meeting, which might serve to isolate them from the masses of other middle-class, white, southern Protestants. A majority of them, although by no means all, do have ancestral ties to the county where the campground is located although a significant number of them no longer reside there. They seem not to think of themselves as a group as opposed to other groups. On those rare occasions in conversation when it is necessary to make a distinction between themselves and those of their relatives, friends, or neighbors who do not participate in the camp meeting they simply refer to themselves as "camp meeting people." ("We've been camp meeting people for years.")

It would seem that a camp meeting person is one who camps at the camp meeting, but the term encompasses more than those who actually camp. The Tentholder's Association, which is the governing body of the campground, takes an annual census in which it counts every person who spends at least one night at the campground as a camper. This number has varied over the five years I have studied Bethel but averages approximately 350 persons. Clearly this number does not include all of the camp meeting people, many of whom do not camp but attend the services regularly year after year. These noncampers, called "visitors" by camp meeting officials, usually have kin ties with camping families. Visitors often outnumber campers at the services. At the 1984 centennial year meeting there were over 400 campers and over 1,000 persons on the grounds on the first Sunday. These were both records for recent years.

STUDYING BETHEL

On one of my first walks around the bustling campground in August 1980, I made a discovery which has given focus to my study of Bethel. Something caught my eye about one of the tents. Half of the front porch to the left of the front door was made of concrete and the other half of new lumber. A closer look revealed that there was no window on the wall behind the wooden portion of the porch, but there were large hinges on it so that it could be opened like a barn door. A walk to the rear of the tent provided the explanation for this subtle aberration. Carefully hidden behind the facade of the old tent was a modern air-conditioned camp trailer like others I had seen on the grounds but had paid little attention to. The porch had been altered to lift up and the wall to swing open so that the trailer could be backed into place and shut off from view. Further investigation revealed that this was not an isolated case. Several other tents contained hidden trailers and all of the thirty-seven trailers on the ground that year were situated so that they could not be seen from inside the plaza area.

I addressed the obvious question of "why hide the trailers" to the owner of the first hidden trailer I had encountered and her answer seemed to sum up all of the other seemingly vague answers I received on the subject. "Well," she said, "it just seems more like camp meeting that way."

The hidden trailer syndrome, as I came to call it, reveals two important facts about the campground. First, it indicates that the campground as a setting is very important to the camp meeting and that at some level the camp meeting people are aware of its importance, otherwise they would not go to such lengths to preserve it from the encroachment of too much modernity. Second, as this last statement suggests, one important and pervasive characteristic of the campground environment is its archaism. This can be seen clearly in the contrast between the old, weathered, vernacular-style tent and the sleek, modern camp trailer concealed within.

The word archaism is most often used to refer to archaic words or language used on special or ritual occasions and no longer a part of everyday speech. I have used it to refer to archaic forms generally. I have also used the word archaism to refer both to a property of things and to objects which possess this property. Thus something may be characterized by archaism and/or be an archaism.

My first approach to archaism at Bethel was a symbolic one, but it soon became apparent that the camp meeting people did not share my enthusiasm for symbolism. I was forced to conclude that the archaistic campground held no collective, conventional, discursive meaning for camp meeting people. That is not to say that it did not communicate something important, even crucial, to them. It only meant that another approach would have to be taken to decode it.

I decided to pursue a combined cognitive and behavioral approach having both synchronic and diachronic aspects. My first task was to determine what emically defined settings and microsettings existed within the campground environment. Second, it would be necessary to determine what behaviors were associated with archaism in each of these settings and microsettings. Lastly, I would attempt to determine how these associations developed and if they had remained constant through time.

If the behaviors associated with the most archaistic settings could be shown to have changed the least through time when compared with the behaviors associated with the least archaistic settings, then this would imply a possible causal relationship between setting and behavior. In other words, setting could be thought of as an independent variable. The relationship between behaviors and settings could thus serve as a guide in making inferences about what messages are encoded in campground archaism.

THE ENVIRONMENT

I used three techniques to gather data concerning what settings the campers perceived within the campground:

1. I conducted interviews eliciting descriptions of the campground.

2. I asked a group of camp meeting people selected at random to label a small unlabeled sketch map of the campground seen labeled in Figure 15.

3. When engaged in conversation with camp meeting people I remained alert for references to various parts of the campground.

My research revealed that the camp meeting people did indeed have a lexicon of terms for various settings and microsettings within the campground (Figure 1). In fact, several of my informants spoke of how difficult it was to describe the camp meeting and campground to their neighbors and friends who had never been there. In describing it they were forced to use different language. For example, instead of saying they "camped in a tent" they would have to say they "stayed in a cabin"; instead of saying that they "met under the shed" they would have to say that "services were held in the tabernacle."

To the camp meeting people the "circle" (the large plaza formed by the tents) seems to be the setting which defines the entire campground. The shed is said to be in the "center of the circle." Some tents are said to be "on the circle" and some are not. Cars and camp trailers are said to be parked "outside the circle." Based upon this I have schematically depicted the campground as a series of concentric zones (Figure 2).

FEATURES AND BEHAVIORS

Using spatial categories first proposed by Edward T. Hall (1966:-103–129) and later elaborated on by Amos Rapoport (1982:87–101), each campground zone was observed for the presence of fixed features, semifixed features, and nonfixed features. Fixed features are permanent elements and structures within a setting such as buildings. Semifixed features are portable or movable elements within a setting such as furniture, cars, camp trailers, and so on. Nonfixed features are human beings and their behaviors.

Following this scheme, semifixed features were used to control for archaism in each setting. This was necessary because I began with the assumption that the entire campground as a fixed feature is, with some exceptions, an archaism. This being the case, every camp meeting behavior would be associated with archaism, thus making the study moot. Although archaism is a universal characteristic of the camp-

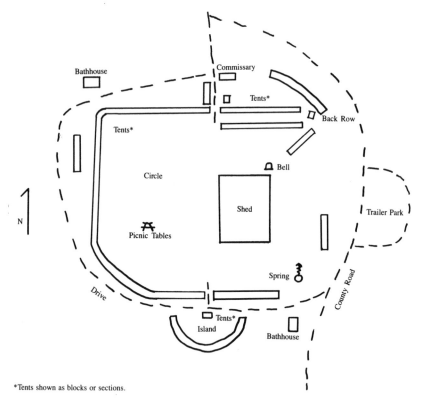

*Tents shown as blocks or sections.

Figure 1
Settings of Bethel Campground.

ground, the semifixed features which are brought to the camp meeting each year are, with a few exceptions, not archaisms. Therefore it was necessary to determine if there was a patterned distribution of these modern semifixed features such that some settings would remain relatively more archaistic than others. In other words, I wished to determine which settings were least intruded on by modernity and which were most intruded on. This was done simply by observing which semifixed features were present in each setting.

The results of this part of the study clearly showed that as one moves from the periphery of the campground toward the center archaism in-

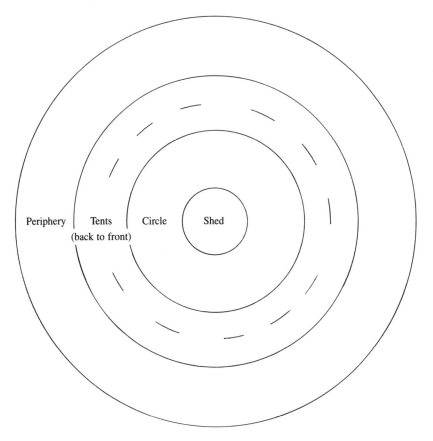

Periphery | Tents (back to front) | Circle | Shed

Figure 2
Campground Settings as Concentric Zones.

creases rather dramatically. Although none of the campground settings is entirely free from modern semifixed features they are overwhelmingly more frequent in the peripheral zone.

This is particularly true for large, obtrusive features such as automobiles and camp trailers. No automobiles are parked within the circle. Once the meeting has begun, they are only allowed in the circle temporarily for special purposes such as unloading elderly visitors at the shed. No camp trailers are allowed within the circle unless they are concealed within tents so that they cannot be seen from the shed.

Until the 1984 encampment none of these proscriptions had the force of law. They were informal rules which had evolved, according to my informants, to "preserve the camp meeting spirit." Those who violated the rules risked being talked about, and this was apparently a very effective social control.

TENTS FRONT AND BACK

It is not possible here to discuss the complete inventory of semifixed features and associated behaviors for every campground setting. However, because it has both on-circle and off-circle microsettings, a brief examination of a typical on-circle tent will reveal the basic pattern of distribution for both features and behaviors in the major campground zones.

Tents are owned by families. They may be handed down from generation to generation, bought, sold, or rented. If a tent is not used for a number of years or is in a bad state of repair it may be condemned by the board of trustees and either torn down or given to another family. At camp meeting time tents are usually occupied by extended family groups or at least augmented nuclear families. They also serve as a home base for noncamping relatives and close friends of the family.

As fixed features all tents on the grounds share a number of characteristics. They all have tin roofs and are all built of rough unpainted lumber. They all have electricity and have had since the 1950s; however, none has plumbing, screening, or glazing. They are all built in one of several vernacular styles which were once common to the area. Most predate 1940; the oldest dates to the 1890s. They are continually being patched up or in some cases totally rebuilt, but even new tents are built to conform to the characteristics described above. The only modern innovation which has begun to appear in recent years is the concrete slab floor, but such floors do little to alter the outward appearance of a tent and are not considered intrusive.

With very few exceptions there are three microsettings within each tent: the back porch (out of the circle), the interior room or rooms, and the front porch (in the circle). The differences in the distribution of semifixed features and associated behavior between these three micro-settings indicate that the tents on the circle form a transitional zone between the periphery and the circle.

It is on the back porch, which serves as a kitchen, where the greatest number and variety of modern semifixed features are encountered. In frequency of occurrence these range from refrigerators to microwave ovens (refrigerators being most frequent).

Parked automobiles and camp trailers are clearly visible from the back porch. In fact, some families park trailers directly behind tents to supplement sleeping space. In some cases everyone may sleep in the air-conditioned trailer, take their meals on the back porch, and walk through empty rooms to sit and visit on the front porch. In such cases, the tent's role as a conduit into the circle can be clearly seen.

The back porch is definitely a feminine domain. Traditionally men sit on the front porch in the evening while women prepare meals on the back porch. When the meal has been eaten, men return to the front while women clear the table and wash up.

The room or rooms between the porches of the tent are used for sleeping, dressing, and storage. This interior space is sometimes parti-tioned into two areas either by fixed or temporary dividers or as com-pletely separate rooms. In the past, according to camp meeting tradi-tion, males slept in one of these areas and females slept in the other. However, today if there is any division it is between adults and chil-dren. The rooms are furnished with beds, perhaps a small table, a small dresser or chest-of-drawers, and curtains on the windows. Most of these items are cast-offs from home where they are stored and used only for camp meeting. In some cases they are old camp meeting heir-looms passed down through families. The most modern semifixed fea-ture likely to be found in this area is an electric fan.

Stepping out onto the front porch one completes the transition from back to front, outside to inside, and enters a more traditional and time-less environment. From the front porch the entire tree-canopied circle is visible. It is possible to see what is going on at the shed and on all of the other front porches.

Almost every front porch has a swing, which is the preferred place to sit. If a person is not fortunate enough or fast enough to claim a place in the swing, he or she must then sit in a folding lawn chair or perhaps on a rough wooden bench, also common features on front porches. When guests arrive they are usually offered the swing, especially if they are women. Some swings are used at home and taken down and brought to camp meeting, but most are carefully stored from year to year. Many camp meeting people say they have neither place nor occasion to use them at home. Only a few camp meeting people live in houses having functional front porches. Swings are definitely valued archaisms.

A front porch on the circle is a box seat on a social arena. People may sit on their front porches and visit with neighbors sitting a few feet away on the next front porch. They might chat with people "making the circle" or share a glass of tea with guests.

Front porch conversation is generally concerned with reminiscence or catching up on what has happened with friends and relatives since the last meeting. However, two subjects which are never discussed are politics (even in election years) and religion.

Religion at Bethel is almost entirely confined to the shed. It is permissible in porch conversations to comment on performance aspects of the services such as how long-winded the preacher is but not on substantive aspects such as the sermon topic. The reluctance of the Bethel people to talk about these matters very much resembles what James Fernandez (1965:907) refers to as a "patterned avoidance," and its purpose seems to be the same—that of preserving social consensus.

Traditional forms of social interaction are found almost exclusively inside the circle where archaism is best perserved. Religious activities occur under the shed, children play in the circle, and adults visit on front porches. Behaviors such as buying and selling, cooking, eating of ordinary foods, maintenance of hygiene, and excretory functions are confined to the peripheral zone. Activities in the peripheral zone are more like activities of everyday life and are surrounded by the trappings of everyday life.

Activities in the circle, however, are shielded from contemporary semifixed features and are considered special and unusual. In the outside everyday world the camp meeting people do not attend religious services twice a day, and for the most part the ones they attend on Sunday are different in both substance and style from the old-time religion under the shed. Neither do they spend much if any time at home visiting with friends on the front porch or enjoying a game of horseshoes. Most of their time at home is spent in air-conditioned interiors watching television.

THE PROCESS OF ARCHAIZATION

A study of oral history and documentary sources such as the minutes of the Tentholder's Association from 1902 to the present has revealed that the Bethel campground has not always been an archaism. In its earliest days the campground setting more nearly matched everyday settings. In fact, many people were first introduced to important new technologies such as automobiles and electricity at the camp meeting. In 1924 electric lights were run to the shed powered by a gasoline generator. This was almost twenty years before electrical service was readily available in the area.

Sometime after 1935 great shifts in population and in the economy occurred which brought rapid change to the everyday lives of the camp meeting people. The area lost population during the Great Depression and World War II (United States Bureau of the Census 1952). The mechanization of agriculture and the coming of industry to the area in the 1950s brought further change.

The camp meeting population peaked in the 1920s and began to decline. However, a significant core of local people remained faithful and kept the meeting going even as other campgrounds in Arkansas closed never to reopen (Baugh 1954).

It was in the 1930s that the process of archaization (here defined as the process by which a form becomes an archaism) began. This process began by chance as a by-product of other forces. Expansion of the campground simply ceased in the 1930s. No new tents were built, but like all material objects the existing tents had a certain permanence. Some were abandoned and subsequently torn down, but most survived. In 1935 there were 126 tents. Today there are 89 tents, the majority of them built before 1940. The cessation of expansion, the object permanence factor, and Bethel's physical separation in time and space from the rapidly changing everyday world of the camp meeting people permanently froze the campground setting in the vernacular traditional world of pre-1940 rural Arkansas. Gradually the campground became a place where remnants of a traditional lifestyle were preserved. Instead of a setting for yearly revival meetings the campground was becoming the object of a pilgrimage where people paid homage not only to their religion but to a way of life they saw rapidly slipping away.

By the 1960s archaization was complete so that when camp trailers first appeared in the latter part of that decade they met the resistance of Bethel's fully matured archaism. The result was the development of the hidden trailer syndrome described earlier. Recently the camp meeting people have become increasingly self-conscious. They are aware of the uniqueness of the camp meeting and the campground and have now taken steps in the form of official rules to preserve it. The culmination of this new self-awareness was the 1984 centennial celebration with its emphasis on the history of the camp meeting and the campground.

Many celebration activities had the effect of enhancing the archaism of the circle. Kerosene lamps were hung under the shed and used at the night services instead of electric lights. "Fire towers" were built around the outside of the shed with small pine knot fires on their tops to provide additional lighting. Many people, including the preacher, wore old-fashioned clothes to the Sunday services. One of the tents built around 1924 was turned into a museum depicting life at the campground before 1930. A trough for storing milk was restored to the spring.

Front/back behaviors at Bethel in the prearchaistic period prior to 1940 closely resembled the front/back behaviors of everyday life. A 1933 history theme written by a local high school student after her first visit to the camp meeting stated that "the houses [tents] are all well built and comfortable, the likeness of home, with every convenience for cooking and eating" (Moores 1933).

In the back (outside the circle) at camp meeting meals were cooked on wood stoves; food was preserved on ice, in spring water, or on the hoof (chickens and milk cows were brought to the meetings); baths, when taken, were taken in large galvanized tubs filled with spring water which were allowed to sit in the sun to warm. The same types of behavior are performed in the back today but in drastically different ways so that the resemblance to everyday home life has remained constant.

Present front activities at Bethel as described earlier appear to closely resemble those of the past and to differ greatly from present-day at-home front behaviors. Thus at Bethel front (inside the circle) behaviors have remained more constant in association with greater archaism of setting while back behaviors at camp meeting have kept pace with changes in everyday home life and are associated with less archaism of setting. This of course suggests that the archaistic setting inside the circle serves in some way to elicit traditional forms of social interaction. In sum, the most traditional behaviors at Bethel occur in the most archaistic, invariant, and, to the camp meeting people, most sacred settings (Figure 3).

CONCLUSION

In his nonverbal communication approach to meaning in built environments architect-anthropologist Amos Rapoport states that "it is clear that in terms of the effect of environment on behavior, environments are more than just inhibiting, facilitating, or even catalytic. They not only remind, they also predict and prescribe. They actually guide responses, that is, they make certain responses more likely by limiting and restricting the range of likely possible responses" (1982:78).

Rapoport suggests that settings communicate by inference. People infer from settings what the rules are for behavior and act accordingly. He further states that "for it to work inference must be easy to make and should be made in the same way by all those involved, hence the need for cultural specificity, clarity, strong noticeable differences, adequate redundancy, and so on. . . . In general, successful settings are precisely those that successfully reduce variance by clear cues and consistent use, which increase their predictability" (1982:79). He suggests the word "legible" to describe such settings.

Thus archaism would seem to be that which makes the campground legible to the camp meeting people. It is the invariant cue within the camp meeting setting which continues to elicit traditional forms of social interaction. The camp meeting people have achieved what James Fernandez (1965:913–914) has identified as a social consensus based not on shared meaning but on shared action elicited by a commonly held signal. In the case of Bethel Camp Meeting it is a shared and invariant setting which serves to trigger behaviors which produce consensus.

Archaism and invariance have another interesting correlate at Bethel,

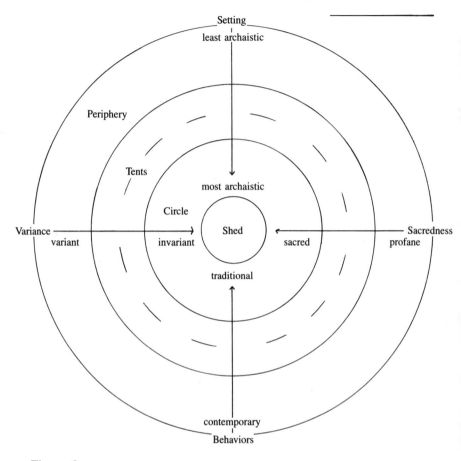

Figure 3
Campground Correlations.

that of sacredness. Roy Rappaport (1979:208–211) has suggested that sacredness is derived from the invariance of ritual. This view is similar to that of Maurice Bloch (1973), who also sees a link between invariance, sacredness, and the archaism which results from the extreme formalization of ritual speech, singing, and dancing. Bloch (1973:76–79) suggests that such ritual archaisms have little discursive meaning for ritual performers. They are more important for what they do, according to Bloch, than for what they say, and what they do is to validate traditional authority.

The findings of this study are consistent with both Rappaport's and Bloch's views except that at Bethel sacredness and invariance can be seen as aspects of ritual setting as well as of ritual performance. This first became clear to me when I attended the Love Feast service at the 1980 encampment. The Love Feast is a communion service held once each camp meeting. After the women in charge had led a hymn and a prayer and read scripture and before the home-baked bread and the cup of spring water were passed, testimonials were called for. Many in the small congregation testified and, almost to a person, each began his or her testimonial with these words, "I love this campground." They spoke freely about how sacred it was, often linking it to events in their personal and family histories. Then one elderly woman stood and, pointing across the circle to one of the tents, said tearfully, "I can still see my mother and father sitting on the front porch and all my brothers and sisters." It was the same front porch across the same circle from the same shed she had known for seventy years. It is doubtful if any other setting in her experience has remained so stable and invariant.

To the camp meeting people the outside contemporary world has become increasingly hostile to the traditional social interaction found at Bethel. The campground has thus become a refuge of sorts for them—a place where they truly feel at home. According to Mircea Eliade "religious man" desires always "to live in the sacred" (1961:28). For the people of Bethel always is not possible but ten days out of every August have become a necessity.

REFERENCES

Baugh, Stanley Thompson, 1954. *Campgrounds and Camp Meetings in South Arkansas* (Little Rock Ark.: Little Rock Conference of the Methodist Church).
Bloch, Maurice, 1973. Symbols, Song, Dance, and Features of Articulation: Is Religion an Extreme Form of Traditional Authority? *European Journal of Sociology* 15:55–81.

Boles, John B., 1972. *The Great Revival, 1787–1805: The Origins of the Southern Evangelical Mind* (Lexington: University Press of Kentucky).

Bruce, Dickson D., Jr., 1974. *And They All Sang Hallelujah: Plain-Folk Camp Meeting Religion, 1800–1845* (Knoxville: University of Tennessee Press).

Dieter, Melvin Easterday, 1980. *The Holiness Revival of the Nineteenth Century* (Metuchen, N.J.: Scarecrow Press).

Eliade, Mircea, 1961. *The Sacred and the Profane* (New York: Harper and Row).

Fernandez, James W., 1965. Symbolic Consensus in a Fang Reformative Cult. *American Anthropologist* 67:902–929.

Hall, Edward T., 1969. *The Hidden Dimension* (New York: Anchor Books).

Hill, Samuel S., Jr., 1966. *Southern Churches in Crisis* (New York: Holt, Rinehart and Winston).

Johnson, Charles, 1955. *The Frontier Camp Meeting: Religion's Harvest Time* (Dallas, Tex.: Southern Methodist University Press).

Jones, Charles Edwin, 1974. *Perfectionist Persuasion: The Holiness Movement and American Methodism, 1867–1936* (Metuchen, N.J.: Scarecrow Press).

McLoughlin, William Gerald, 1978. *Revivals, Awakenings, and Reform: An Essay on Religion and Social Change in America, 1607–1977* (Chicago: University of Chicago Press).

Moores, Martha, 1933. *Customs of the Campground* (manuscript in the files of the author).

Rapoport, Amos, 1982. *The Meaning of the Built Environment: A Nonverbal Communication Approach* (Beverly Hills: Sage Publications).

Rappaport, Roy, 1979. *Ecology, Meaning, and Religion* (Richmond, Calif.: Atlantic Books).

United States Bureau of the Census, 1952. *Census of the Population: 1950*. Vol. 1: *Number of Inhabitants* (Washington, D.C.: U.S. Government Printing Office).

Commentary

James L. Peacock

This symposium represents an exciting union of archeological, historical, and ethnographic inquiries that serve both to deepen knowledge of the Southeast from the sixteenth through the twentieth centuries and to further methodological and theoretical discussion. I shall briefly review the papers before suggesting one or two general points.

Our knowledge is extended backward chronologically by Charles Hudson's ingenious reconstruction of a sixteenth-century world of tribal chiefdoms encountering explorers who are themselves barely emerging from the Middle Ages. George Sabo's suggestive symbolic analysis of a particular Indian/European encounter, the Caddoan, usefully complements Hudson's overview. Hester Davis' search for a Cherokee site in Arkansas carries us forward in time to the nineteenth century. Leslie Stewart-Abernathy's reconstruction of the Moser farm and Cynthia Price's reconstruction of Ozark frontier communities round out a picture of the nineteenth-century southwestern Southeast. This picture—given a rather peaceful tone by the archeological reconstructions—is shaken by probes of two kinds of conflictful events: lynchings of blacks, recounted painfully by Burton Purrington and Penny Harter, and the removal of Indians, which Melanie Sovine (who unfortunately was not able to submit her paper for publication) tellingly revealed to be connected to the missionary and anti-missionary movements. The analyses of the Chinese store by Mary Jo and William Schneider and of the camp meeting by James Rees compellingly demonstrate "structural" patterns salient in parts of the Southeast to the present.

The symposium, then, is crafted to provide coverage both of southeast ethnohistory since European contact and a range of methodologies in ethnohistory, from the archeological to the archival to the structural. The organizer and the authors deserve congratulations for an excellent and useful symposium.

As a way of carrying forward reflection on ethnohistory as an approach, whether applied in the Southeast or elsewhere, two omissions might be noted which may reflect emphases (and underemphases) not only in this symposium but in the paradigm guiding ethnohistory in general. These emphases reflect, I suspect, the identity of ethnohistory with science more than with the humanities, an identity which (as Hudson notes) derives from the intellectual history of anthropology.

The symposium gives relatively little attention to native texts while emphasizing modes of analysis which treat the natives as silent objects, whose patterns of living must be reconstructed by the observer from information other than written reflections by the natives themselves. Archeology must reconstruct lifeways of Ozark Cherokee or whites from sites and artifacts; historians must write about lynchings of blacks from records left by persons other than the blacks themselves; Chinese storekeepers and camp meeters are shown to follow structural patterns or occupy structural positions through analysis of spatial and spatio-social classification schemes rather than through written reflections. These nontextual analyses are, of course, designed to balance the over-reliance of the historian on the journals and other writings of the elite literati—the Southern aristocrat and his ilk in Southern historical studies.

But it seems that an important source of data falls between the stools of history and ethnohistory. This information is neither the written reflection of the elite nor the nonwritten residue of the folk. It is information provided by a stratum that is highly literate but not elite, a folk culture grounded in text and textuality to a striking degree. I have in mind from my own research a certain Primitive Baptist elder from Appalachia. A stonemason boasting only a seventh-grade education, he had memorized the King James Bible and absorbed the writings of John Bunyan and was conversant with the seventeenth-century British theologians influential in forming the doctrine of his church. This elder, now in his seventies, has written a remarkable autobiography, which is one example of many others by Primitive Baptists. Of the authors contributing to this symposium, Sovine made most use of this kind of information; it is a source that could be more deeply plumbed as ethnohistory explores its relationship to history.

The second suggestion comes from a comment by Hans-Georg Gadamer regarding Hegel. Gadamer writes:

He [Hegel] shows his clear grasp of the futility of restoration when he writes of the decline of the classical world and its religion of art that the works of the Muses "are now what they are for us—beautiful fruits torn from the tree. A friendly fate presents them to us as a girl might offer those fruits. We have not the real life of their being—the tree that bore them, the earth and elements, the climate that determined their substance, the seasonal changes that governed their growth. Nor does fate give us, with those works of art, their world, the spring and summer of the ethical life in which they bloomed and ripened, but only the veiled memory of this reality." (Hans-Georg Gadamer, *Truth and Method* [New York: Crossroads, 1982], p. 148.)

Gadamer reminds us what we already know all too well, that complete and pure reconstruction of the past is impossible. All that we can do is reconstruct the past in relation to the present, our present. Therefore, we should include as part of our explication of history the explication of this relationship.

This familiar lesson, easy to state but difficult to apply, should not be interpreted as advising ethnohistorians of the Southeast to emulate those historians of the Old South who write history as an apologia for the Lost Cause. Even less should we be driven to turn history into a grimly phenomenological introspection that forgets sites and events in favor of dissection of the self. Still, a modicum of self-reflection would seem a sensible and necessary facet of an ethnohistory which recognizes that any reconstruction achieved expresses both the data gleaned from the past and the experience and perspective of our present. Here the humanistic roots of history could fruitfully balance the positivist scientific models of ethnohistory.

Whatever suggestions may be set forth, the reader cannot but be impressed by the strength and promise of the ethnohistorical endeavor as grounded here in the southeastern region and represented by these particular papers. For anthropology in its incessant search for a guiding model, ethnohistory provides a workable and compelling union of important methods and perspectives. Ethnohistory may indeed demand, as suggested by Hudson's stirring call to arms, a strategic role for anthropologists working in the Southeast.

Contributors

HESTER A. DAVIS is state archeologist at the Arkansas Archeological Survey and professor of anthropology at the University of Arkansas. She conducted fieldwork among the North Carolina Cherokee in 1955–56 while a graduate student at the University of North Carolina, Chapel Hill. As part of her current work on management and conservation of cultural resources she is interested in the archeology of early nineteenth-century Cherokee settlement in Arkansas.

PENNY L. HARTER obtained her bachelor of arts degree from Southwest Missouri State University in secondary education with an emphasis on social sciences. She was also National History Day Champion at Billings High School, Missouri.

CHARLES HUDSON, professor of anthropology at the University of Georgia, is well known for his many studies of southeastern Indians. Recently he has devoted considerable effort toward retracing the route of the de Soto expedition through the Southeast and using the accounts of early Spanish chroniclers to reconstruct aboriginal social and political organization.

JAMES L. PEACOCK is professor of anthropology at the University of North Carolina, Chapel Hill. A specialist in symbolic and psychological anthropology, he has conducted fieldwork in southeastern Asia as well as in the southern United States.

CYNTHIA R. PRICE is research archeologist at the Southeast Missouri Field Station of the Center for Archaeological Research, Southwest Missouri State University. She has been involved in ethnohistoric and historic archeological research in southeast Missouri for more than a decade. Much of this research has focused on nineteenth-century pioneer settlement and subsistence adaptations in the eastern Ozarks.

BURTON L. PURRINGTON, professor of anthropology at Southwest Missouri State University, has had extensive involvement in archeological and ethnological research in the Ozark and Appalachian regions of the South. He is a specialist in cultural ecology and rural societies and is currently involved in research on turn-of-the-century race relations in southwest Missouri.

JAMES A. REES, JR. teaches social studies in an experimental program at Springdale High School, Arkansas. His research interests include southern camp meetings and religion and the anthropology of education.

GEORGE SABO III is associate archeologist at the Arkansas Archeological Survey and assistant professor of anthropology at the University of Arkansas. He has done archeological and ethnohistoric research in the Canadian Arctic and in the Ozarks and is especially interested in relations between Native Americans and early European explorers.

MARY JO SCHNEIDER is professor in the Department of Anthropology at the University of Arkansas, Fayetteville. Her special interests are applied anthropology, southern culture, and sex roles.

WILLIAM M. SCHNEIDER is an associate professor of anthropology at the University of Arkansas, Fayetteville. His areas of specialty include social organization, religion, structuralism, southeast Asia, and American culture.

LESLIE C. STEWART-ABERNATHY is associate archeologist at the Arkansas Archeological Survey and assistant professor of anthropology at the University of Arkansas. A specialist in historical archeology, he has excavated numerous sites in Massachusetts and Arkansas. Current research interests include urban studies, ethnicity, cognition in economics, and the social history of technology.